DOWNFALL
Lessons for Our Final Century

DOWNFALL
Lessons for Our Final Century

Ilhan Niaz

CSCR | CENTRE FOR STRATEGIC AND
CONTEMPORARY RESEARCH

اداہ برائے تزویراتی و عصری تحقیق

CSCR | CENTRE FOR STRATEGIC AND
CONTEMPORARY RESEARCH

ادارہ برائے تزویراتی و عصری تحقیق

Centre for Strategic and Contemporary Research
Second Floor, Ace Venture Plaza, Street 5,
Service Road North, E-11/2, Islamabad - 46000
+92 51 2712221 | editor@cscr.pk | www.cscr.pk

Preferred Citation:
Niaz, Ilhan. *Downfall: Lessons for Our Final Century*. Islamabad: Centre for Strategic and Contemporary Research, 2022.

ISBN 978-969-7828-04-3

Typeset in Garamond
Published by
Centre for Strategic and Contemporary Research

ACKNOWLEDGEMENTS

Thanks are due to Ejaz Haider and Riaz M. Khan for providing feedback on earlier versions of some of the essays in this volume. I am profoundly grateful to my parents, Kamran and Nuzhat Niaz, and my wife, Uzma, for reading these essays as they were being written. I am also indebted to Ailiya Naqvi and the wonderful team at CSCR, which includes Talha Ibrahim, Fareha Iqtidar, Hassan Zaheer and Aurangzaib Khan, for helping bring these essays into publication. I alone am responsible for any errors and omissions.

CONTENTS

Preface

The following essays were written in 2018 and 2019, preceding the COVID-19 pandemic. The ongoing global health emergency, while terrifying, significantly tested human ingenuity, compassion, and resilience. The relatively successful way in which countries with minimal resources, like Vietnam, Bhutan, Sri Lanka, and Pakistan, have coped with the crisis contrasts sharply with the heavy fatalities incurred by the European and American populations that enjoy a wealth advantage of 30 or 40 to 1 over countries in the Global South. At the same time, East Asian societies, irrespective of political dispensations, have generally fared better than others due to effective state response and greater social discipline. Owing to the rapidly evolving nature of the virus and the challenges that remain in terms of vaccination and treatment, it is fair to say that COVID-19 is going to be a part of our collective life for decades to come. The virus is a warning from nature that humanity needs to heed. Our destruction of the world's natural habitat, our insatiable demand for access to exotic species with which we should not have contact, and our dependence on fragile globalised supply chains, are the factors that have brought us to this dreadful ordeal. There is now an irrefutable case for moving towards an ecologically regenerative economy built around the minimal exchange of goods and strictly necessary travel over long distances.

Sadly, even amidst this crisis, governments, corporations, and plutocrats are keen to get back to business as usual. Some are hoarding vaccines, and others are accumulating great fortunes on the backs of soaring demand for digital services. Society is confronted with a flood of disinformation motivating vaccine hesitancy and a sheer denial of the existence of COVID-19. The virus and the pandemic are a cruel Darwinian test of our fragmented sense of reality, be it derived from modernism, post-modernism or traditionalism. The virus does not care what anyone's regime of truth is - it will decimate any society that refuses to make necessary adaptations. The greatest weapon that the virus wields is that it turns our human need to be with other people and our propensity to think ourselves immune to disaster against us.

Indeed, humans are generally not good at contemplating the end. It is an unpleasant exercise in relation to oneself or loved ones. Our minds rebel against such efforts, and society strongly discourages such melancholic endeavours. Never losing hope is a cardinal principle of religious faiths, modern ideologies, and the vacuous self-help industry. Capitalism legitimises itself by propagating rags-to-riches stories, millions opt into lotteries, and in almost every major cultural entertainment product, good guys win in the end. Soldiers are trained to never say die, sportspersons are conditioned to keep playing till the last minute, doctors are mandated to do everything possible to prolong human life, the young are taught to feel invincible, and the old are encouraged to feel and look young. Therefore, it is not surprising that states and societies have a hard time thinking rationally about the future, and they behave as if they will last forever.

It is perhaps for this reason that students of history often find themselves at odds with the wilful denial, self-deception, or sincere delusion that characterises the behaviour of most individuals and collectives. History teaches us that all things have a culmination point, that no state is permanent, and that individuals are transient and expendable. It trains us to see the world, historically, in terms that reveal a dead past of structures and mentalities that continue to live and an evanescent present that continuously dies. The humbling fact is that the ultimate test is that of time, and time always wins.

The essays that follow have been written with a very heavy heart that is weighed down by the mounting evidence that life on Earth has been plunged into mortal danger by modern human civilisation, particularly the neoliberal variant of capitalism that has raged and dominated globally over the past 40 years. The damage already done is so great that a crisis of habitability is inevitable. And our heedlessness is so entrenched that humans, especially the top 10 per cent, will continue to plunder and waste until the Earth becomes unfit for all life. This downfall is, in historical terms, underway with early-onset disasters starting to assert themselves. The Global North, with its wealth and technology, might survive a little longer. The Global South will probably collapse somewhat sooner. But however one cuts it, the end of modern civilisation as it is presently understood is likely to unfold between 2030 and 2100.

If humanity, in general, and the Global South, in particular, is to have any chance of surviving the great churning headed in its direction, everyone needs to greatly add to the presently limited reserves of wisdom. The seven essays that comprise this anthology are an effort to draw lessons from history and philosophy and relate them to the present crisis. Though voices from the Global South are generally not taken seriously on any matter, and global issues are reserved for the commentary of metropolitan elites, it is hoped that this small effort to provide some perspective from Pakistan, a country that has done very little to contribute to the impending disaster but is nonetheless going to bear the brunt of it, might prove useful to policy makers, environmentalists, and the general public.

It is also my hope that every prediction made in the pages that follow is proven wrong and that the scenarios envisaged do not come to pass.

Ilhan Niaz
Summer 2022
Islamabad

Introduction: The Anatomy of Downfall

When historians approach an event or a period, they have to choose, sometimes from a range of options, a beginning, a middle and an end. For instance, if we were to write about Europe's Dark Ages, we could begin the story at AD 476 (the end of the Roman Empire in the West) or AD 312-320 (the transfer of the capital to Constantinople and the conversion of the emperor to Christianity), or AD 180 (the death of Marcus Aurelius and the end of the *Pax Romana*). The point where one chooses to start a story will affect the structure of its main body and its eventual conclusion. Civilisations and empires emerge from obscurity, rise to glory through a series of trials and tribulations, achieve their zenith, and then decline and fall. They leave behind knowledge, beliefs, and cultures picked up by others who march on for a while before they too are replaced. For as long as history and philosophy have existed, thinkers have wondered if there is any grand design to the historical process or any meaningful outcome that will emerge from the sum of all human exertions. The philosophy of history is, in particular, concerned with attempting to detect and explain patterns and, in some cases, speculate as to the ultimate results. From a contemporary perspective, it does seem as if an answer to these great questions can be given. Sadly, the answer is that the present grand design will reach a culmination, and human civilisation will literally destroy the planet by 2100. Its story will come to a terrible end and be accompanied by the ruination of the Earth's ecosystem so absolute that no comparable civilisation will be able to arise for thousands of years. This was not the final result that Vico, Hegel, Comte, or Marx expected, nor is it what the neoliberal globalists thought would happen when they proclaimed history to be over with the fall of the Soviet Union and saw the future as a triumphal march of free markets and democracy muddied only by self-inflicted instability arising from boredom. The far darker perspectives of Herodotus, Ibn Khaldun, Malthus, Mill, Spengler, and Toynbee, appear to have come closer to explaining reality. But even they did not see the possibility of an uninhabitable world emerging due to human activity.

Since the early 1990s, the globalist promise that all people could get rich and free with limitless growth for all has maintained the hegemony of heedless optimism. Today, it is as if more and more people, even in the West, are waking up from a long slumber, finally jolted by a level of ecological destruction that is impossible to ignore. The anger at globalist elites is palpable. They sold the world on the lie that infinite material growth was possible on a finite planet. They managed the lie so poorly that even in rich countries, inequality spiked, and the welfare state shrank, creating a backlash within the metropolitan core of globalism. And, having exhausted many of the world's resources and destabilised the vital chemical, biological, and thermal processes upon which all life on Earth depends, the level of poverty, in relative terms, has defied meaningful reduction for much of the world's population with over 40 per cent of humanity still unable to afford adequate nutrition. So, under the influence of growth cultists, advocates of globalisation, and the enforcers of corporate capitalism, a great unravelling of the rich tapestry of life on Earth in the form of the human-caused Sixth Mass Extinction is entering a mature and irreversible phase. In view of the totality of the collapse that the world faces, it is incumbent upon those engaged in the study of history to explain why humanity has failed so dreadfully when it comes to heeding the scientific advice on environmental issues for nearly 50 years. Staring into the abyss that lies ahead is necessary since it is the product of human actions and failures. The only way to avoid actually falling into it is to rationally comprehend how it came to exist in the first place.

Gaining a better understanding of what is happening and where the world is headed is even more important for people from the Global South, for whom the cruelty and injustice of environmental collapse are particularly severe. This severity is due to the fact that the people of the Global South had to foot most of the bill for the rise of capitalism, globalisation, and the modern world. From the Atlantic slave trade and the genocide and expropriation of indigenous peoples in the Americas, Africa, and Australia, to the systematic draining of resources from dominions of conquest (like India) and the unfair trade practices imposed on others, the wealth of the West is largely stolen from the rest.

Without the tremendous subsidy reaped by Western economies from plunder and extermination of these indigenous communities through its colonial projects, the gap between the Global North and South would be a lot narrower. Even at present, with an arguably rules-based trading system, the Global North extracts an annual surplus of nearly 2.3 trillion dollars from the South. It is no surprise, therefore, that the wealth gap between rich and poor has grown - within and between societies. Due to industrialisation, the bulk of the Greenhouse Gas (GHG) emissions since 1800 have also been produced by states in the Global North. The scale and intensity of industrialisation were themselves functions of draining resources and capturing markets from indigenous peoples and Asian and African lands. Precisely because the Global North has hoarded and multiplied its ill-gotten wealth, it is better placed to mitigate the effects of the ecocide that its consumption has unleashed. For the Global South, mitigation is not as feasible because many of its countries are already warm, most of its people are too poor to afford expensive coping strategies, governments are too disorganised and unstable, and local globalist elites have more to gain in the short-term by facilitating the plunder and unequal global exchange that is promoted by neoliberalism.

Even with the onset of climate apartheid and the highly uneven losses that the ecological disintegration is likely to generate (at least for another 30-40 years), environmental awareness in the Global North has risen dramatically since 2000. Campaigners such as the United States former Vice President Al Gore; movements like the Extinction Rebellion; bureaucracies such as the United Nations (UN); and Non-Governmental Organisations (NGOs) such as Green Peace have helped shift the public discourse in favour of environmentalism in the developed world. The basic message that these, and many other entities, have hammered home is that the simultaneous disruption of many of the Earth's natural processes due to human activity is going to land everyone in an inescapable mess. What is not surprising about these movements is that the white middle and upper-middle classes of the developed world dominate them. Few people of colour and fewer voices from the Global South are actually getting through.

Having created a problem on account of the historical accumulation of crimes against other peoples and the natural world and having aggravated that problem through sheer greed since the 1970s; the younger generation in rich countries is beginning to recognise the brutality of the colonial enterprises of their ancestors and the historical guilt associated with the legacy they inherited from them. Consequently, woke white people, alongside metropolitan people of colour, have found a new great cause – saving the world "from themselves, for themselves". A new chapter in white guilt is being written, which in consonance with previous chapters, emerges after the fact only, does nothing actually to compensate victims in any substantive sense, and does not prevent the commission of further crimes.

What such pangs of guilt do lead to is tokenism and rebranding. If a government feels under pressure from ecological extremists, it can declare a climate emergency. If politicians think that young people in rich countries are anxious about maintaining or improving their living standards in a future of ecological ruin, they can announce a Green New Deal. If local governments feel they must do something about environmental pollution, they can ban single-use plastic bags. If international organisations feel that popular resistance to their ill-advised cut-and-paste solutions is about to boil over, they can start talking about "inclusive" growth.

Even conservative governments, like the one in the United Kingdom, can try to co-opt the Extinction Rebellion rhetoric by announcing net-zero targets for 2050 while threatening protesters with legal and police action for daring to disrupt business-as-usual. Individuals can make carbon pledges, forswear the use of materials that are not biodegradable, and reduce their air travel. These measures are nonsensical from the perspective of the Global South, which is running out of time to address the consequences of climate change and ecocide. They are but a psychological coping mechanism to help the principal collective perpetrators of ecocide (the Global North) feel better about themselves so that when poor countries start to implode under the pressure of environmental collapse, the benevolent white folk and their resident diversity representatives can feel that at least they tried to make things better.

Western leaders know this full well that the climate models in use significantly underestimate the rate of global warming and do not adequately account for the feedback loops that are already being generated. Hence the recent alarm at observing that the Arctic ice melt has reached levels in 2019 not expected till 2090 or that biodiversity loss in the form of mass extinctions of insects is proceeding far more rapidly than anticipated threatening the continuity of the processes upon which the agricultural cycle depends. It is naïve to think that the Global North will execute an ecological revolution within the next nine years that will save the Earth. The best that can happen is that rich countries will set in place climate mitigation measures and attempt to ride out the storm as its worst effects consume the Global South.

Pakistan, which contributes less than one per cent of global GHG emissions and has a per capita consumption of resources so low that at its standard of living, it would take a global population of 16 billion to exceed the Earth's carrying capacity, is a case in point. Due to its geographic location, generally arid environment, and demographic distribution, it is one of the 10 most vulnerable countries when it comes to climate change. Likely to run out of water by 2040 and burdened by a rapidly growing population, Pakistan spends barely 0.3 per cent of its Gross Domestic Product (GDP) on research and struggles to achieve universal primary school enrolment. An important cause of Pakistan's dire demographic profile is that since 1947 it has been locked in conflict with its giant neighbour, India. In spite of impressive GDP growth rates since the neoliberal economic reforms in 1991, India, like Pakistan, is also among the worst ecologically affected countries.[10] While India and Pakistan literally fight over melting glaciers, the energy they deploy against the real enemy, i.e. regional environmental collapse, which does not care about national borders, is minimal. Indians will not be able to drink their foreign exchange reserves, just as Pakistanis will not be able to eat their nuclear weapons, once regional habitability evaporates, along with most of the water, in another 10-20 years. If India and Pakistan have any plans to still be around in 2100, they need to put aside their "strategic" confrontation and devote all efforts to a survival plan rooted in regional cooperation.

As options narrow and time runs out, many are becoming desperate for solutions, falling into despair, or channelling their energies into activism. Before a realistic solution can be arrived at, it is necessary to understand the causes of the problem. Central to the challenge that lies ahead is that human technical and scientific progress have so far outpaced social, psychological, and biological evolution.[11] Humans are very smart, but they are hardly ever wise enough to think in the long term. Easily distracted by shiny objects, modern humans have collectively deluded themselves into thinking that indefinite and infinite material growth is possible on a finite Earth. Our entrepreneurs, corporations, bureaucracies, and manufacturers are adept at calculating the prices of goods and services without factoring in the real environmental costs of producing more and more GDP.

Therefore, this anthology is an effort to generate a discourse on the continual failure of human society to think about its survival in the future amidst the impending climate catastrophe. It is intended to make us rethink our contemporary approaches toward confronting significant climate challenges. This anthology, grounded in history and philosophy, comprises seven essays that distinctly frame contemporary ecological crises with respect to different dimensions of the problem and tries to offer a different vision for how the world could collectively deal with it.

The first essay explores the ideas of Ibn Khaldun, Malthus, John Stuart Mill, and Darwin in determining what the future holds and what modern society ought to draw from the past. The rationale behind making it the first essay is to dissuade the readers from the popular and historically inaccurate rhetoric that present crises are unpredictable.

The second essay addresses the modern obsession with economic growth and how it has contributed to the ecological crisis. The difficulty the world's leaders and economists have in envisioning a world without GDP growth indicates that a profound dearth of ideas besets mainstream politics and economics. Most economists and development practitioners do not have the faintest clue as to how wrong the central assumptions of their disciplines are or the massive contradictions that lie beneath the surface of the ocean of economic sophistry in which policy makers and leaders have been drowning for decades. Liberation from the irrational tutelage of growth cultists is essential to humanity's survival.

Ensuring survival will also require humans to make much better decisions oriented towards long-term outcomes. The third essay uses Herodotus and his *Histories* to probe why humans are terrible at making wise decisions. The ability to distinguish between wise and unwise is vital if humanity is to avoid making bad decisions in panic or simply trying to continue as before out of hubris.

One of the most powerful factors that fuel hubris is optimism, and this is the subject of the fourth essay. Taking the arch-optimist Professor Pangloss from Voltaire's *Candide* as the exemplar of positive thinking, the weaknesses of this approach are dissected. The luxury of time allowed humans to indulge their optimistic tendencies in the past. At present, time is rapidly running out, and it is imperative that rational and practical thinking unencumbered by wishful weak-mindedness guides the future course of policy. This clarity is necessary if states are going to endure through the apocalyptic ecocide induced geopolitics that awaits the world in 20 – 50 years' time.

The fifth essay explains the implications of the climate apocalypse for international relations. As the world heats up in temperature, it is also going to heat up in terms of inter-state conflict. The winners and losers of the looming struggle will not be like the victors and vanquished of many past conflicts. This time, the losers will cease to exist.

Those alive today are living through the last days of a global civilisation in a high-level equilibrium phase. This makes it difficult for them to grasp the excruciating reality of the transience and fragility of their opulent lifestyles and the imminent danger of downfall. As the sixth essay argues, the downfall is the inevitable result of an intensive and unequal developmental model highly reliant upon rapaciously extractive economics. The trouble is that this time the global reach of extraction has undermined the ability of the Earth to support complex life. The globalist high civilisation is going to end in global collapse with all major cultures at risk of extinction along with most of nature.

The final essay examines what types of political orders might emerge during and after the collapse of the Earth's habitability. In the medium term, the most likely outcome is a new wave of fascism, while the most benevolent outcome is a wave of relatively mild environmentalist dictatorships. In the long run, tribalism, survivalist movements, and small-scale isolated communities in especially favoured locations are likely to be all that is left of human societies by 2100.

Let us then proceed to the first stop on this journey to learn some lessons for what is shaping up to be our final century.

I

Lessons for Our Final Century from Ibn Khaldun, Malthus, Mill, and Darwin

> History is a discipline widely cultivated among nations and races. It is eagerly sought after. The men in the street, the ordinary people, aspire to know it. Kings and leaders vie for it. Both the learned and the ignorant are able to understand it. For on the surface, history is no more than information about political events, dynasties, and occurrences of the remote past, elegantly presented and spiced up with proverbs…The inner meaning of history, on the other hand, involves speculation and an attempt to get at the truth, subtle explanation of the causes and origins of existing things, and deep knowledge of the how and why of events. History, therefore, is firmly rooted in philosophy. It deserves to be accounted a branch of it.[1]
>
> – Ibn Khaldun (Arab Philosopher, Historian, and Sociologist, b. 1332, d. 1406)

Ever since Herodotus and Thucydides wrote the first critical and explanatory histories, the subject of the rise and fall of civilisations has fascinated historians and philosophers. The imperial or civilisational breakdowns of the past were almost invariably local and regional, with a few notable exceptions, such as the Mongol eruption of AD 1200 – 1400, which was global in consequence. It was only about 500 years ago that a genuinely global human civilisation could be said to have emerged. Primarily driven till 1945 by the agency of Western imperialism, this process is now transitioning to a period of Eurasian globalisation centred on China and India.

The age of globalisation has produced improvement in the quality and quantity of human life. On average, the human lifespan has doubled over the past 150 years, with much of the gain in the last 70. Even societies like those in South Asia or Africa, considered poor or underdeveloped, are vastly wealthier and more productive than 100 or 200 years ago. The contemporary material aspiration for practically all societies is to achieve a standard of living comparable to the old, industrialised states of the Western civilisation. And in pursuit of this goal, economists have perpetuated a cult of economic growth eagerly echoed by political leaders who, whether elected or not, understand their primary role as improving economic conditions for their people. The path to this desirable outcome, economists assure us, is through increasing the size of our economies, taxing enough to pay for essential services and infrastructure, and providing incentives for growth. Confronted by increasingly inescapable environmental limits to their preference for growth, some have taken to mouthing glittering phrases like "sustainable development", "grassroots empowerment", "green growth", "inclusiveness", and "knowledge-based economy". Like Professor Pangloss from Voltaire's *Candide* (more on him in the fourth essay), they remain convinced, in spite of all experience to the contrary, that we are living in the best of all possible worlds and that somehow technical innovation and more disciplined enforcement of environmental rules will allow us to advance along an infinite growth trajectory.

The sustainable development paradigm is a hoax. Its advocates are either sincerely mistaken or charlatans, profiting from selling placebos to help with a dread disease. Many of them are genuinely unable to draw logically consistent conclusions from the irrefutable evidence that our planet is dying and that it is our insatiable greed that is killing it. On a more extreme level of delusions, some fantasists advocate becoming an interplanetary species or hold out hope that science and innovation will find a way out of the mess – that the rise in environmental awareness will, in the near future, turn us all into good ecologists. Far from enduring long enough to colonise other worlds and harvest their resources or terraform them to habitability, human civilisation is almost certain to self-terminate by making its home planet uninhabitable by the end of this century.

Awareness will not help either. Consider recycling – in spite of broad awareness in the industrialised world, we only recycle about a tenth of plastics and dump the rest into our oceans or in landfills.[2] The result is that by 2050 there will be more plastic than fish in our waters. Further, consider childcare products.[3] People claim to love their children, and they do at an emotional level. But, knowing that disposable items are destroying the planet and making a decisive contribution to the onset of humanity's extinction event, which is likely to unfold in their children's lifetime, will not convince many parents to stop using disposable diapers or plastic bottles or baby formula without viable alternatives.[4]

Contemplating how and why things end is not easy, but four key thinkers can help us understand probable futures. The first of them is the 14th century Arab philosopher of history, sociologist, and political economist, Ibn Khaldun and his intriguing perspective on how regimes fail to maintain rationality in decision-making. The second is an 18th century English economist and demographer, Thomas Malthus, who posited his idea on the problem of population growth in relation to the planet's natural carrying capacity. The third is a 19th century English philosopher, John Stuart Mill, who theorised on what would happen to our world if the growth stage of economic development continued indefinitely and the resulting desirability of an eventual stationary state. And the fourth thinker is a 19th century English biologist, Charles Darwin, whose classical work in evolutionary biology propounded on the exposition of the natural forces that lead to the evolution of life and how the basic mechanisms that drive this process are likely to lead humans to commit fatal errors.

Ibn Khaldun's views on the origins of life and speciation foreshadowed Darwin, and his understanding of human nature and mentality approximated or exceeded Enlightenment and even modern analyses. Ibn Khaldun was particularly concerned with the problem of political order. History indicated to Ibn Khaldun that empires rose and fell in cycles accompanied by changes in the rationality and enterprise of ruling elites. Concerned primarily with dynastic states and the historical experience of West Asia and North Africa, Ibn Khaldun offered an explanation for this cycle of growth and decay. The basic mechanism that enabled state formation was a sense of group feeling (*asabiya*). Group feeling was strong when a community was faced with challenges and threats that imperilled its immediate survival. Dire circumstances necessitated that individual interests be subordinated to the collective good. Consequently, heightened group feeling was strong amongst tribal, nomadic, or semi-nomadic peoples that lived on marginal terrain and in harsh environments. The trouble was that this primordial group feeling, while it made for tight-knit clans or kinship groups willing to die for each other if needed, also made large-scale cooperation between such groups difficult. It was only through religion or ideology that such a society could temporarily transcend internal rivalries and unify. When that happened, such peoples could overrun agrarian heartlands and become the rulers of sedentary societies.

Insofar as sedentary societies were concerned, the experience of group feeling was different and, in critical respects, weaker than that of nomadic societies. For starters, sedentary societies were too numerous for everybody to know everybody else. Then, greater material comfort and insulation from the kind of hardship endured by nomadic cultures enabled the members of sedentary societies to pursue a self-centred lifestyle and selfish ambitions. With a state to protect them, houses to shelter them, trade and markets to enrich them, and refined culture to distract and entertain them, sedentary societies possessed much more of what was materially desirable. But, their relative ease of existence made such people less hardy and more attuned to individual interests. The problem, from the perspective of political order, was that running a high-quality state required courage, determination, pragmatism, and ruthlessness in furthering the common good. When a state elite became infected by excessive self-aggrandisement and material decadence, it started to decline. And in that context, nomadic groups temporarily united by religious ideology could conquer sedentary civilisations, become a new ruling elite, and, for a couple of generations, govern in a relatively effective manner. As the decades passed, however, the rulers would acquire the mentality of sedentary peoples and become decadent, selfish, and incapable of providing leadership – thus restarting the cycle all over again.

Ibn Khaldun explained the effects of power and wealth on rationality and the tendency of ruling elites to degenerate into corrupt and self-serving oligarchies or autocracies. Viewed in the context of long-term survival, it was not in the interest of any ruling group to acquire qualities that would lead to its downfall and the collapse of its host society. The trouble was those very wealthy and powerful people were almost invariably carried away by the trappings of their success and came to view themselves as innately better than others. This sense of entitlement, explained by Ibn Khaldun as the misguided belief in nobility as an inherited rather than acquired attribute, destroyed the rationality of ruling elites and led them to make decisions that might make them richer or more powerful for a while but ensured destruction a few decades down the road. While modern polities are, at least in the West and parts of East Asia, no longer overtly dynastic or tribal in the way that they were in AD 1400, the effects of power on mentality have remained fascinatingly unchanged. We see this in the consolidation of plutocracies and secretive corporations aware of the long-term effects of mining the environment but driven by the more immediate need to ensure the next quarter's profit. They use their immense wealth to warp political processes to suit their immediate economic interests. It is no surprise, therefore, that just 100 companies have, since 1850, accounted for over half of GHG emissions and put some 1.1 trillion tons of carbon dioxide into the atmosphere (since 1988).[5] And they are not going to stop because a Swedish teenager made a stirring speech at a climate change conference in Poland. It is evident that globalisation has produced a global service and corporate oligarchy that is incapable of reform.[6] Instead, since the 1980s, it has doled out half-baked compromises and promises of "sustainable" development for propaganda purposes. As for the members of the public, we are all culpable because few of us are prepared to accept restrictions on our consumption patterns or standard of living for the sake of the environment. Most of us want to save our planet, provided that it does not entail personal inconvenience or sacrifices. The sheer absurdity of delegations travelling by carbon-intensive methods, like aircraft, to attend conferences on climate change (or other environment/eco-babble fests) is lost on those engaged in such enterprises.

Ibn Khaldun realised that humans, as a species, are fundamentally unjust and want to behave selfishly; while deluding themselves that this does not make them bad actors. While our desire to believe in our uprightness even as we pursue what suits us to the detriment of others and the survival of the planet lies at the root of our cognitive dissonance, providence and nature require logical consistency and cognitive integrity for long-term survival. Elites that make decisions that destroy the very planet they live on, and citizens that buy into the belief that growth can be sustained indefinitely on a planet with dwindling resources, represent the kind of behavioural pattern associated with a civilisation on the verge of collapse. This kind of behaviour falls within Philip Zimbardo's definition of evil as knowing better while doing worse.

Thomas Malthus's 1798 foray into future studies, *An Essay on the Principle of Population*,[7] aimed at challenging notions that humanity could somehow remove all material difficulties in the way of achieving utopian conditions. The idea of progress, common to many Enlightenment thinkers, did not apparently have a cap. Though some, like Adam Smith, even argued that the fruits of the pursuit of selfish interest were somehow redistributed by an invisible hand. Malthus argued that while he hoped the optimists were right, there was a fundamental constraint on our material wellbeing, and that was the carrying capacity of our planet. He bifurcated his idea into two rates – geometric and arithmetic, respectively. He wrote that the human population, under favourable conditions, grew at a geometric rate, while our ability to extract more from our environment, to grow more food, etc., grew at an arithmetical rate. What this meant was that every breakthrough that allowed us to feed or support more people led to population increases that soon outstripped improved productivity.

This, in turn, forced us to find ways to further increase output. We could bring more land under the plough, colonise new territories, intensify the exploitation of existing resources, etc., but the more efficiently we did this, the faster our population would grow, leaving us gasping eternally for breath to escape the effects of our own ingenuity. Malthus framed two basic hypotheses from this insight. One was that improved production would, due to escalating population pressure, leave the vast majority of people in relative or absolute misery at a bare subsistence level. The other was that our ability to grow more to feed ourselves would ultimately run into hard natural constraints and fail. Malthus's insights, for nearly 200 years, appeared to be confounded by innovation. The world that Malthus lived in had perhaps one billion inhabitants. Today, the world has nearly eight billion people, likely to rise to nine billion by 2050. Much of this increase has occurred since 1945 and can be attributed to a reduction in the death rate owing to advances in medicine, increased commerce and global trade, and rising incomes in developing countries. Life expectancy has practically doubled over the past century, meaning that people consume resources for a lot longer than they used to. Increasing per capita consumption[8] also means that people consume resources at a greater rate. And there is hope that breakthroughs in growing food in labs and other biotechnological advances may well allow us to feed more people and keep them alive for even longer. However, the downside of all these technological innovations is that the energy required to grow food and the resources required to sustain modern civilisation will keep increasing. As Jason Hickel has noted, the total carrying capacity of the Earth in terms of resources renewed by natural processes is about 50 billion tons a year. At present, human civilisation consumes 70 billion tons a year.[9]

If we have a global Green New Deal, as the leaders of the Extinction Rebellion want, then, by 2050, humans will be consuming 95 billion tons of resources a year. If we continue with the current growth model, then by 2050, humans will consume 180 billion tons of resources a year. Even the Green New Deal advocates, all well-meaning people, ironically want to grow the economy sustainably, so entrenched in the public mind is the ideology of growth preached by generations of economists. Even if human civilisation goes green, it will still destroy the planet – after all, those rare earths needed for solar panels and other smart technologies[10] are not going to be mined or shipped by themselves. No matter how we plan our next moves, our planet's ecosphere is headed to collapse, driven by plummeting biodiversity and climate change under any extractive economic model compounded by increasing consumption and rising numbers of people. Malthus's bleak view of the future is all set to reassert itself with a vengeance. Bluntly put, there are simply too many humans living too long and consuming too much for the Earth to sustain for very much longer. A Malthusian correction of apocalyptic dimensions is a probable and increasingly proximate outcome of the damage humans have inflicted on the Earth's life-support systems. An important cause of our impending Malthusian correction is our inability to think about modern political economy in terms other than growth – a significant absence of an alternative idea of a political economy. Political leaders continue to promise growth and feel that their legitimacy is tied to increases in Gross National Product (GNP). Economists assure us that growth is good and that we are all better off as a consequence of it. Yes, there are debates about equity, relative inequality, sustainability, terms of trade, and inclusivity, but the underlying assumption is that growth must continue, even if it leads to the collapse of our planet. It also needs to be pointed out that today, according to the World Bank, Gross World Product (GWP) per capita is about 17,000 dollars (in terms of Purchasing Power Parity (PPP), and were it to be distributed fairly, then without any further addition to Global GNP, we could provide every human being with a decent living.[11] But that is not going to happen because well off people in the Global North (with per capita incomes in the range of 30,000 – 50,000 dollars) are not going to give up 40-60 per cent of their incomes so that South Asian peasants, who live on a 1,000 dollars a year if they are lucky, can be bumped up to decent middle-income status.[12] And the few hundred billionaires who account for half of the global wealth are not going to fork over their plunder unless subjected to confiscatory policies by states – states whose political elites have been bought and paid for by the very plutocrats driving our planet towards collapse.[13] John Stuart Mill's monumental *Principles of Political Economy* contains a concise but profound reflection on the eventual outcome of economic growth. Written half a century after Malthus, by which time the industrial revolution was in full swing in Western Europe, Mill wondered about the "ultimate point" of industrialisation. Mill hypothesised that in order to save the planet from exhaustion, the growth-oriented stage would have to be replaced by a "stationary state". This condition could arise once humans had accumulated enough wealth to enable everyone to live moderately well. By imposing restrictions on inheritances, regulating wages, and redistribution of wealth, broad equality of economic outcomes could be ensured within which variations in individual prosperity would arise from enterprise, not inherited privilege or property.[14]

The purpose of economic growth, Mill felt, should never be the mere accumulation of materialistic longings. Rather, the purpose ought to be to enable people to live well enough so that they have enough leisure to pursue the things that they want to. Once society was wealthy enough to achieve this outcome, it no longer needed to keep adding to its GNP. Instead, it could continue to make things better through innovation and the accumulation of knowledge divorced from any specific profit motive. Such a society, Mill reasoned, would be sustainable in the long run. Mill warned that the alternative to the termination of economic growth in a stationary state was a "world with nothing left to the spontaneous activity of nature; with every rood of land brought into cultivation, which is capable of growing food for human beings; every flowery waste or natural pasture ploughed up, all quadrupeds or birds which are not domesticated for man's use exterminated as his rivals for food, every hedgerow or a superfluous tree rooted out, and scarcely a place left where a wild shrub or flower could grow."[15] A century and a half after Mill's dire warning, humanity is close to achieving this lonely, desolate, outcome. In confusing "more" with "better", humanity is all set on being left without an ecosphere worth the name by the end of this century.

The Darwinian paradigm helps explain what had happened in the past when species had to adapt to macro changes in the objective conditions around them. Darwin's primary framework, as articulated in *On the Origin of Species by Means of Natural Selection* (1859)[16] and *The Descent of Man* (1872),[17] has been greatly expanded in the past 150 years. Advances in palaeontology and genetics enable us to understand the processes of evolution far better than Darwin could have ever hoped for. At the same time, popular science fiction movies, such as the *Jurassic Park* franchise, have explored in wondrous cinematic detail the possibility of directly controlling evolution and bringing back extinct life. This being said, we are far more likely to go extinct ourselves before we bring the Tyrannosaurus Rex back to life. And the reason for this is textbook Darwin – nearly all life that has ever existed has gone extinct. Nature has, over time, killed off 99 per cent of life on Earth.[18] All the creatures that existed at the dawn of hunter-gatherer human societies represent a hundredth of all life to have existed on the Earth. Darwin's framework identified five critical ways in which this struggle for survival played out. First, life seeks to replicate itself and requires the consumption of energy from the environment around it. Organisms, in other words, have to eat. Second, life adapts to highly specialised niches, which enables it to secure a steady supply of energy and minimises competition for that resource. Once equilibrium is found, life likes to stay put for as long as possible. Third, once in a stable niche, those traits that enable more efficient extraction of resources become desirable and advantageous attributes that are more likely to be passed on to the next generation. Successful adaptations are sexy, and those who manifest them are likely to produce more offspring. Evolution then rewards those adaptations by giving them more energy allocation. Fourth, depending on the specifics of environmental circumstances, a single species can evolve into many different ones, and many species can converge. Fifth, any sudden change in objective conditions will leave most creatures in the lurch, unable to adapt, and vulnerable to extinction.

Attributes that are a big advantage in one set of circumstances can become severe disadvantages under another. That is how mammals, who were small rodent-like creatures for 100 million years (160 million – 65 million BC), were better placed than the dinosaurs when that meteor struck Earth. Large reptiles that needed lots of food could not survive the post-apocalyptic conditions after the meteor hit. On the other hand, small, warm-blooded, nocturnal, semi-troglodyte mammals were able to survive. And once the dust settled and the dinosaurs were no more, mammals exploded into the vacuum, adapting to new niches and conquering the world. At present, human activity has destabilised the world's ecology and is causing mass extinctions of animals, plants, and, as is becoming evident, insect life, all of which are vital to the maintenance of the ecosystem that we depend on. Human beings are really smart. Our brains have been the key to successful adaptation to a wide variety of environments. The more our ancestors used their brains to manipulate the environment, the more numerous they became and the further they spread. And once, about 10,000 years ago, agriculture began enabling sedentary cultures, and by 4000 BC, civilisations emerged, and the human presence on the planet exploded, as did its ingenuity. In a mere 6000 years, humanity went from the Stone Age to the Space Age. And while this was good, in the sense that people lived better, longer, and more sophisticated lives, it also meant our demand for the planet's resources soared. The energy-intensive civilisations of the past six millennia were, and are, phenomenally expensive to maintain. In order to keep going, they mined the environment, spread in territorial extent, waged wars, enslaved less materially advanced cultures, eradicated other large animals and human populations, and figured out ways to increase productivity through trade and technology.

The past 250 years have seen the intensification of this mining process to a point where it has made the Earth very ill. One symptom of that illness is climate change – particularly global warming. Like a body fighting an infection, the Earth's temperature is increasing. As the Earth heats up, humans' entire chain of energy extraction becomes more costly to maintain and vulnerable to disruption. However, human beings are so blinded by a hubristic reverence for their own ingenuity that we are prepared to do everything except reduce our total consumption to the point consistent with the Earth's carrying capacity. Our intelligence is no longer a survival advantage. It is, in fact, a disadvantage. If we were a lot less intelligent and had never advanced beyond hunter-gatherer bands, we would be living nasty, brutish, and short lives. But our species and our planet's ecosphere would survive for millions, perhaps hundreds of millions, more years. Instead, like Adolf Hitler in his command bunker during the last year of the Second World War, we remain convinced that a miracle device or other fortuitous development will see us through to victory over the dark future. As humanity becomes more desperate to survive amidst the ruins of its planet, it is likely to employ intelligence to do unimaginably stupid things. One such thing would be messing around with our genetic code in order to genetically engineer ourselves into surviving on planet Mad Max. Another would be to invest massive amounts of resources from our dying world into trying to become an interplanetary species. Yet another would be for countries armed with weapons of mass destruction to unleash those assets on less powerful states in a bid to secure control over remaining resources. A remote possibility could be some sort of geoengineering solution whereby we start tossing chemicals to cool our atmosphere from above to allow us to keep pumping more carbon dioxide into it from below. Or, better yet, let us introduce mechanical life animated by Artificial Intelligence (AI) into our collapsing ecosphere and see how that works out – such life would be ideally adapted to surviving long after the Earth has become unfit for organic life. Essentially, our future is likely to be extinction or a post-human dystopia that will make nightmarish works of science fiction appear almost benign.

Let us recap the lessons we can learn about our present and future from Ibn Khaldun, Malthus, Mill, and Darwin. In terms of politics and administrative order, human civilisation is in the grip of plutocratic control, regardless of the formal political system. The decadent and self-aggrandising behaviour of the global elite, which seeks to keep in place the system that is the source of its wealth and privilege, has left human civilisation in an advanced stage of selfishness, decadence, and senility. We simply do not have the political will to make the harsh decisions needed to save our species and planet. In terms of demographics, the human population is going to continue to grow and ravage natural resources until they run out. Our extractive ability will continue to improve until there is literally nothing left to take. Malthusian constraints might be delayed, but they will not be denied and bite all the harder when they set in. On the economic front, in the absence of a stationary state emerging soon, growth will continue to be the priority. No matter how one cuts it, growth driven by consumption, trade, and manufacturing will cause the collapse of the ecosphere. Going green will buy us time, but it will not secure salvation for us. It does not appear remotely possible to eradicate the ideological cult of economic growth. And then, there are the evolutionary implications of what we are doing. Our large brains cannot accept that it is our very intelligence that is undermining our chances for survival to the next century. Human activity is destabilising the ecosphere, and the fantastical solutions being dreamed up by optimists are more likely to accelerate humanity's terminal crisis than offer a real solution. Blaise Pascal got it right when he said, "We run carelessly to the precipice, after we have put something before us to prevent us seeing it."[19] At this stage, even if we manage to see things clearly, it may well be too late for course correction.

Growing to Oblivion:
The Crisis of Economic Thought and Our Final Century

The Earth is a living planet and the source of all known life. Arguably, there is no task more urgent and more sacred than to care and preserve this crucible and home of life. We are also witness to the ravages done to the planet by humans who alone have the capacity to reverse the damage which has been caused by unbridled consumerism spurred by avarice and unrelenting manufacturing on the wheels of industrialisation and expanding technological capacities. Today, human activity in the production and manufacturing sector employs capacities far exceeding global needs. The service sector which is also as old as human economic activity provides efficient distribution of goods and enhances quality of living conditions. But today this sector is increasingly locked into the productive sector to accelerate and expand their mutual capacities. Instead of balanced and justifiable growth, the two sectors often create superfluous needs for each other's profit. Human energies ought to be channeled in an arena which provides useful employment for enhancing the quality of life in rhythm with nature and without expanding productive activity and placing stress on the natural environment and global resources. [sic][1]

– Riaz Muhammad Khan (Pakistan's Foreign Secretary, 2005-8)

Economists and their political acolytes believe in growth. Whether one examines Adam Smith or Karl Marx, John Maynard Keynes or Milton

Friedman, or Steve Keen, self-serving plutocrats and globalist hacks or wide-eyed champions of a Green New Deal, or the perspective of global institutions like the World Bank, International Monetary Fund (IMF), or the UN, the all-consuming obsession is with growth. Of course, within economics, there are outliers like Thomas Malthus or John Stuart Mill, and there are a number of non-economists, like Jared Diamond[2], Yuval Hariri[3], and Peter Turchin[4], who realise, or had realised, that our planet's carrying capacity imposes ultimately hard limits on growth and that it is not a good idea to push beyond those limits. But few political leaders, finance ministries, and corporate elites take what these critics of growth have to say seriously. There is the usual handwringing about increasing inequality, tragic memes on social media about creatures going extinct, and a broad encouragement of environmental awareness. Still, the discipline that feeds bad ideas to leaders and decision-makers remains remarkably impervious to any adjustment to reality. Indeed, economists seem to think it is the job of reality to conform to their fantasies cleverly masked, as they are, by esoteric language, signs, and numbers.

Adam Smith, legitimately regarded as the founder of modern economics, provided the basic blueprint for the idea of growth. To Smith, growth entailed an increase in the wealth of individuals. The combined increase in the wealth of individuals would lead to the enrichment of the national (or imperial) polities they lived in. The wealthier individuals became, the better it was for everyone as, through the pursuit of personal gain, society would become more efficient at producing wealth. This wealth would lift all boats and, through the invisible hand, ensure the distribution of rewards in a manner proportionate to productivity and enterprise. Conversely, those who failed in this competition would do so on account of insufficient productivity or innovation and thus deserve to fail. This failure would also enhance efficiency, and in time the operation of the market would generate increasing wealth for everybody. In the context of this perspective, the role of the state was to provide an enabling environment so that people could, through the rational pursuit of their self-interest, make themselves richer. Thus, the state ought to regulate property rights, maintain law and order, and even provide some education, but its interventions had to be limited in scope.[5] Even today, the growth cultists adhere to these basic tenets and believe in the inherent rationality of selfishness, the basic correctness of market mechanisms for allocating resources, and moral acceptance of inequality as being the legitimate outcome of free and fair competition.

One political economist and philosopher of history by the name of Karl Marx, had a serious problem with the inequality that the market economy produced. He was outraged by the misery of the proletariat, the obscene display of wealth by the robber barons, the obvious unfairness of the state in rigging the game against the poor and in favour of property and privilege, and the psychological toll of mechanised alienation from life itself.[6]

His central insight was that the existence of a system of property ownership is the root of all this evil and that history is merely the narrative account of a profound structural tension between the few who own property and the many who do not. The solution lay in redistributing the fruits of growth evenly, and this could only be achieved by the collective ownership of property or communism. Communism would allow growth and prosperity to flourish as never before, and then everyone would have a stake in the wealth of the society they lived in. Though Marx envisaged communism as being the result of industrialisation, the societies where his ideas first inspired successful revolutions (like Russia and China) were agrarian and backward. They thus formulated a communist path to rapid economic growth (centralised economic planning) accompanied by a relatively even distribution of wealth that managed to appear competitive for a few decades before sputtering to a halt, having inflicted terrible loss of human life on the unfortunate inhabitants of these socialist utopias.

The leading capitalist powers were sufficiently terrified by the apparent success of the Soviet model during its first 50 years that they introduced welfare reforms aimed at keeping their working and middle classes loyal and advocated central planning of economies in developing countries. But the fact is that the communist variant of growth was every bit as ecologically ruinous and unsustainable as the capitalist variant and these two otherwise antithetical frameworks were in a competition to show the world how to grow faster, bigger and better.

The great synthesiser of capitalism and communism and, arguably, the saviour of the former was John Maynard Keynes.[7] Having lived through the First World War and its socioeconomic aftermath, Keynes sought to save capitalism from itself. Prior to Keynes, the classical thinking in economics was that governments ought to cut their expenditures to avoid going deeper into debt as their tax receipts declined in the event of an economic contraction. In other words, in times of economic distress, governments ought to pursue austerity. Keynes blew this idea out of the water and demonstrated that it was precisely when the economy went into a recession that public spending ought to be increased. By producing liquidity and spending it on goods and services, the government would help raise the level of effective demand. This would limit the downward part of the cycle and return an economy to the path of growth quicker than cutting government spending and waiting for the market to correct itself. In theory, increased government spending could keep an economy operating at near full employment, which would cause wages to rise, demand for goods and services to increase, and GDP to keep growing. But the magic started to wear off in the late-1960s as the generation born after 1945 came of age. This generation had benefited greatly from the relatively equitable growth between the years 1945-1968. Unlike their parents, who had lived through two world wars and the global economic depression, this generation came to believe that its extraordinary good fortune was the product of some innate qualities rather than favourable circumstances – a typical human conceit that cannot be quantified for the purposes of economic analyses. This generation also came to think that it deserved to keep getting richer. But, there was a problem. In order to maintain the level of social mobility seen between 1945 and 1968, high taxes were needed. The various restrictions and state interventions in the market over the preceding generation were deemed stifling. During the wars of Containment, the slowing of growth and political scandals discredited the established political and economic leadership. And the stage was set for a generation that had benefited more than any in human history from public interventions in the economy to become addicted to the myth of its rugged individualism and a neoclassical or neoliberal economic ideology that justified kicking aside the ladder and trampling upon what was left of the ecosphere in the pursuit of private profits. In the 1940s, as the Age of Keynes headed towards its greatest accomplishments, a reactionary movement aimed at returning to a purer free-market interpretation of economics took hold at the University of Chicago. Considering themselves anti-Keynesian, Milton Friedman and his apostles of free-market fundamentalism would take the world by storm in the 1980s. Their ideas still constitute the bedrock of contemporary neoliberal economic thought. The core scripture of this movement is Friedman's *Capitalism and Freedom*.[8]

The essential argument (made in a way that can be understood non-mathematically) is that the market, if allowed to perform without impediment, will achieve optimum efficiency in the allocation of resources. Conversely, the more a market is rationed, controlled, taxed, regulated, or otherwise subjected to non-economic factors, the worse it performs. Thus, for instance, high taxes on the wealthy, from this perspective, discourage investments and entrepreneurship, undermining the growth potential of a society. Welfare payments or subsidies for education, health, or housing, entail state interference in the market and thus reduce economic efficiency. State ownership of assets, especially productive ones, is the ultimate crime against the prosperity of society. Restrictions on trade such as protectionist regulations, high tariffs, or subsidies for local industries also constitute a threat to prosperity and need to be minimised or phased out. Wealth would naturally trickle down if promarket policies were pursued while the economy would expand. The elegance of this hypothesis is that it is supremely value-rational. To anyone who has been conditioned into believing that the market is inherently more efficient than other ways of distributing resources and generating wealth (or calculating wellbeing), any historical or empirical inefficiency in economic functioning can be explained as arising from the interference of non-economic or non-market forces in economic decision-making. This hypothesis also had an obvious appeal to elites in the capitalist world. They could justify the dismantling of the social, legal, and political restraints on the unabashed pursuit of personal financial gain in the name of the greater good and for the cause of restoring economies to competitiveness.

With the threat of communism receding in the late-1980s, this perspective became dominant. Global trade, easing of capital controls, the hyper-dominance of the financial and speculative sectors, the auctioning off of public wealth worth tens of trillions of dollars from one end of the globe to the other, the return of private debt-bondage in advanced economies, the reversal of the 1945-1968 trend towards greater socioeconomic equality, and the growing insecurity of employment, have come to characterise the neoliberal dystopia.

Imagine a world where countries are encouraged to pursue the ecologically ruinous practice of free trade in preference to local production. Imagine a world where levels of relative inequality have returned to what they were on the eve of the First World War. Imagine a world where a few dozen of the richest have as much wealth as nearly four billion poorer people. Imagine a world where people are working longer and harder for relatively less. Imagine a world where 100 large corporations account for 70 per cent of GHG emissions while governments and environmentalists encourage their citizens not to use plastic straws. And now imagine that those responsible for this outrage congregate every year at Davos to bask in self-reflective radiance while expressing token concern about the ruin of the planet of which they are the principal instigators and beneficiaries. Arguably, our world and civilisation are already in a pre-apocalyptic dystopian condition. Unless human civilisation shakes itself out of its present daze, it will have entered a post-apocalyptic dystopian condition by the end of this century.

The trouble is that the basic idea of growth that animates the present order also infects the critics of that order. The critics of the almost libertarian spirit that drives contemporary capitalism and economic globalism fall into several camps. The first are right-wing nationalists who resent the social and cultural pain produced by the rapid movement of capital and labour enabled by the present variant of globalisation. For these elements, especially in the West, the rise of the civilisation-states of China and India are deeply problematic.[9] After all, in free and fair competition, the West was supposed to win and firmly retain control of the terms of engagement. Changing racial and cultural composition through migration has exposed the limits to which "foreigners" can integrate into White Caucasian cultures steeped in centuries of privilege grounded in the casual de-humanisation of everyone else.[10] In non-Western countries, strongmen and aspiring autocrats or elected demagogues, sensing the seismic shift, want to gain greater control over globalisation and direct it towards the enrichment of their nations. Both seek a greater share of growth for themselves and use identity politics to deflect from the unsustainability and irrationality of the pursuit of GDP increases as a panacea. The Brexiteers, Donald Trump, Xi Jinping, Narendra Modi, Mohammed bin Salman, Recep Tayyip Erdoğan, Rodrigo Duterte, and Vladimir Putin are the most high-profile examples of this phenomenon.

They all want to make their countries great again and provide growth on their terms. The second includes left-wing and centrist critics of mainstream economics. No one paid much heed to them in the late 1990s and early 2000s, but when the Great Recession of 2008 hit, their analyses gained wider popular currency. Some of these thinkers, such as Steve Keen, Anne Pettifor, Raghuram Rajan, and others, had accurately predicted the global financial crisis of 2008.[11] Others like Yani Varoufakis had experienced firsthand the Greek meltdown – how imperious and unrepentant the priests of economic orthodoxy were even in the face of the disaster they had clearly been responsible for.[12] In many respects, these thinkers idealised the Keynesian approach toward stagnation and low wages and were critical of the inequalities that had been heightened by the pursuit of free-market policies and austerity regimes. Their disagreement was not concerned with the desirability of growth but with its equity and with the excessive dominance of financial interests in decision-making to the neglect of the real economy, of people, places, things, and ideas. The third group of critics can broadly be identified as the sustainability crowd. They include many outfits devoted to promoting sustainable economic development, reconciling growth with environmental protection, and lobbying for increased regulation. The very governments and forces that advanced neoliberal prescriptions around the world patronise the most successful of these organisations, which, in turn, act as a friendly opposition to the dominant orthodoxy. Others are hardcore activists and community-based initiatives operating at the local level. Most recently, growing alarm at the rapidly approaching tipping points identified by scientists beyond which limiting climate change and averting ecological collapse will become impossible[13] has led to the Extinction Rebellion[14] and the open advocacy of a Green New Deal.

Countries like China and Germany are pouring resources into shifting from carbon-intensive sources of energy, while others are banning plastic bags, examining biofuels, and advocating "green growth". But here is the rub. Even if human civilisation as a whole move to renewable sources of energy, our total consumption of resources will, by 2050, be twice what the Earth can replenish in a year.[15] Furthermore, the speed with which the complex systems that sustain life on Earth are unravelling makes it highly unlikely that converting to renewable energy will save the planet. It is also unfortunate that even as the share of renewable energy in total output rises, the total consumption of fossil fuels will continue to increase well into the future. This is partly driven by increased global trade. The carbon footprint of freight was about 2.1 billion tons in 2010 and is projected to rise to 8.1 billion tons by 2050.[16] At present, about a 10th of global carbon emissions are due to international trade in commodities and transport.[17] The more we trade and travel, the faster our planet will die. The iron grip of the idea of growth ensures that even as human civilisation presides over the liquidation of its planet, those involved in economics from varied perspectives debate the best way to ensure growth, oblivious to the fact that any and all economic frameworks that require the extraction, movement, and expenditure of resources on the present scale will lead to planetary collapse.

There are theoretical alternatives to growing our way to oblivion. But these alternatives will remain on the drawing board because they run counter to far too many aspects of human understanding and behaviour.

The most important of these is the human understanding and experience of time. For most of us, it is hard to think far into the future as humans innately are a creature of the immediate. In fact, what we consider "far" is not that far in historical terms and minuscule when we relate it to evolutionary, environmental, or geological timescales. Even the wisest person will have difficulty in seriously thinking, in any detail, about what lies more than five or ten years ahead. Some individuals may be concerned with their legacy or with the next generation, but when it comes down to the brass tacks, we are creatures of the moment. The elites who dominate us are also obsessed with the short-term. Corporations pursue their quarterly results. In democracies, leaders face frequent election cycles that average between two and six years. In the media, the daily car crash gets most of the coverage, not the approaching apocalypse. Universities and think tanks, often working off corporate or donor-sponsored agendas and funds, rarely encourage serious long-term reflection and certainly offer few, if any, incentives to facilitate such exertion. Even the most enlightened autocracy or harmonious society (China as the contemporary exemplar of the former and Japan and Denmark as instances of the latter) will have a hard time thinking more than 50 or 100 years ahead.

Our individual and collective inability to see ourselves in historical time leads to constraints on what we perceive to be threats. The challenge facing the world in terms of environmental breakdown is an inter-generational one that has been building for at least a century. It has accelerated after the year 2000, the year that saw total human consumption of resources exceed, for the first time, the ability of the Earth to replenish itself.[18] But even this acceleration is slow compared to situations that would actually get perceived as dangerous and lead to an appropriate life-saving reaction. Comparisons are sometimes made between the scale of the mobilisation needed to avert the collapse of civilisation due to climate change and the threat of the Axis powers in the 1930s and 1940s. What is often forgotten is that until the very last moment possible, the United Kingdom, France, the Soviet Union, and the United States avoided taking steps to halt the rise of the Axis. It was only after Germany and Japan imposed immediate military danger upon the Allies that they were shaken into taking the steps necessary to ensure their own survival. And here, we are addressing a specific military-ideological threat that came to pose a direct risk to the survival of the Second World War Allies.

This behaviour has not changed, nor will it until it is too late. Since 2001, the United States has spent six trillion dollars fighting the War on Terror in Afghanistan, Iraq, and Syria, and the spectre of terrorist attacks on the American homeland continues to be employed to rally people behind a "security-centred" agenda.[19] The trouble is that terrorism cannot destroy the United States. Climate change can. But the apparent immediacy and lethality of the threat of terrorism is so great and fits in so well with the fear-mongering that politics and the military-corporate convergence feed off that. The state response is skewed towards dealing with a bad headache while the planet is headed towards a cardiac arrest.

So the same United States government that has six trillion dollars to spend on fighting wars to stop terrorism (and has given five trillion dollars in tax cuts to its richest people since 2001), according to the climate change sceptic, Kenneth Haapala, has spent about 40 billion dollars on scientific research into this phenomenon between 1993 and 2014, plus about 105 billion dollars on programs to fight the menace.[20]

Sceptics, like Haapala, feel this is far too much money and subscribe to the crackpot notion that scientific researchers are perpetrating a great hoax and have a vested interest in keeping the climate science dollars rolling in (from this perspective, cancer researchers would be helping spread cancer to keep their research funding levels growing!). But it just goes to show that the United States and most other developed countries have not taken the threat of climate change seriously (as they would an imminent military or security threat). So, our warning sensors are not getting triggered because of the remoteness and lack of specificity in the threat posed by impending ecological collapse.

Another source of numbness to long-term and large-scale danger is that those profiting the most from the status quo have sold the wider public on three myths that make it almost impossible for governments to act decisively. The first is the decentralisation myth that holds that growing awareness and righteous individual and local action can avert disaster. The second is the innovation myth that if we wait just a little longer, we will get the gadgetry to make our unsustainable modern civilisation sustainable. And the third is the win-win myth, which holds that there is no inherent trade-off between environmental sustainability and rising living standards. All three are palpably false, but they reinforce the fundamental human conceit that people are inherently good and that getting materially richer is non-negotiable.

Regarding the decentralisation myth, the sheer scale of the crises of carbon emissions, habitat loss, and diminishing biodiversity facing the world cannot be addressed even if everyone stops using plastic bags and starts eating only free-range chicken and organically grown broccoli while driving around in a Tesla. Imagine how absurd Franklin Roosevelt would have sounded had he, after the attack on Pearl Harbor, urged all Americans to build tanks, destroyers, machine guns, and submarines through their local communities while raising self-supporting local militias that would be shipped overseas to fight the professional armies of the Axis. But this is precisely the kind of absurdity that the decentralisation myth advances and that a great many well-meaning people earnestly subscribe to. "If everyone just does their bit, we will be all right," is a fine attitude in the face of an upsurge in a local street crime or raising money to keep the neighbourhood soup kitchen open. But it does not work when dealing with existential planetary-scale threats, be they the Axis powers or the increasingly proximate collapse of our natural environment.

The innovation myth preys upon the almost universal human desire to solve problems without making any real effort or sacrifice. We are told that new digital avenues will reduce inequality without radical taxation measures or a crackdown on the billionaire class, even though that very class has positioned itself to take maximum advantage of new developments by harvesting our personal data. The brutal increase in relative inequality has been driven in part by new technology that breaks down older and more stable forms of employment. Today's young people work in a "gig" economy, with rising personal debt, unaffordable housing, and tremendous distraction and pressure to "appear" happy and successful via social media. Young people are exhausted by the combination of instability and dopamine-induced narcissism, while the innovations that are alleged to be "disruptive" of the status quo merely reinforce it by manufacturing a context of self-deluding imagery. The innovation myth also conveniently ignores the fact that improvements in the efficiency with which resources can be extracted from the environment inevitably lead to more resources in total being consumed. The problem our planet faces is that the total consumption of resources is far beyond the threshold for sustainability. We will go extinct even if we become far more efficient unless efficiency gains are accompanied by a reduction of at least 50 per cent in humanity's resource consumption.[21] And even such a reduction, which could only be imposed coercively by governments, may not save us because of the amount of damage already done to the Earth's life-support system, the complexities involved being extremely difficult to comprehend in a linear fashion.

The win-win myth is a potent force in politics because it constitutes the dominant element of how public opinion has been shaped to hold self-contradictory positions on the environment. The story goes that every country can be like one of the Group of Seven (G-7) states or Scandinavian. The trick is getting there. In order to get there, you need lots of economic growth. GDP and per capita incomes must rise. Consumption of goods and services must increase. More stuff needs to be produced. And more trade needs to occur. The wealthier a society becomes, the better it is. The job of political leadership is to ensure growth. The costs of this growth, in terms of depletion of resources, are dismissed as unimportant as no one should remain poor. Once a country has caught up in terms of its GDP and per capita, then it can better manage the environmental side of the equation, especially in terms of dealing with local pollution. In rich countries, leaders are afraid to do anything that might reduce standards of living or impose restrictions on consumption. In poorer or middle-income countries, leaders insist that they should not be encumbered by excessive restrictions on how they pursue growth until they can get to the rich category.

What no one is prepared to say is that with a global per capita income in the range of 17,000 dollars (11,000 dollars nominal), we have had enough growth to not need more of it to provide everyone on Earth with a decent standard of living. One can also make the case that in 2000 when nominal GWP per capita (in 2010 constant prices estimate) was approximately 8,500 dollars, and the total consumption of resources had just reached the level that the Earth can renew, had the world economy stopped growing; it could have, with the proper redistribution, sustained advanced civilisation indefinitely and allowed people everywhere to live fairly well. In fact, for the vast majority of the world's people, 8,500 dollars a year is a very good income level. However, rather than taking the environmentally sound but politically difficult decision to even out global wealth, rich countries, in their drive to get richer and reluctance to impose restrictions on their citizens' consumption, simply urged poorer countries to grow their GDP regardless of the stress on the Earth's resources.

Since these myths operate in a mutually reinforcing manner, it is impossible to get the critical mass needed to move states and societies to take necessary actions. These actions would necessarily kill economic growth (whether green or purple) before economic growth kills the planet. The trouble is that hardly anybody is willing to accept that "growth is the problem". Carbon emissions, rising toxicity, habitat loss, plummeting biodiversity, desertification, etc., are the consequences of our reckless pursuit of more GDP.

Instead of more GDP, we need a reimagining of economics in which growth no longer holds any importance once enough wealth has been generated to allow people to live in a fair degree of material comfort. Ideally, this reimagining ought to come from within economics, and, to be fair, John Stuart Mill did envisage a stationary state in which economic growth would cease, and further improvements to life would arise from more leisure and knowledge rather than more work and output.

But economic thought is too invested in the magic of growth. It is not going to reject centuries' worth of its own canon just because a handful of biologists, historians, anthropologists, and environmentalists have woken up to the fundamental problem of the Earth's carrying capacity. The easiest thing in academia is to shrug off criticism from other fields as arising from a lack of subject knowledge on the part of the critics. All sorts of marginal critiques of the mainstream thinking within the discipline can be put forward to tell the critical outsider that they just do not know how diverse the internal debate is. While dismissing critics might make economists feel better, it will eventually leave everyone, including the economists, extinct.

For most of history, economic growth was marginal, linear and subject to reversal. More land could be cultivated. More people could be made serfs or enslaved to farm that land. Precious metals and jewels could be mined and hoarded by states and elites. A militarily weaker neighbour could be plundered or forced to pay tribute. Gift exchange for luxury items might add to the wealth of nobles and wealthy commoners. However, a plague, crop failure, invasion, or rebellion, could wipe out gains made over years or even decades of good fortune. A catastrophe might overtake an entire civilisation sending it into a dark age or wiping it off the face of the Earth altogether.

Recovery, in the former case, would take centuries. Thus, Europe probably did not return to prosperity and social development levels comparable to the Roman Empire in AD 200 until AD 1500. History, therefore, offers us the clearest insight into what a post-growth world might look like if corrective measures are not undertaken and natural corrections arising from planetary resource depletion, ecological collapse, and warfare over dwindling resources take hold. Human beings would, in that condition, move from their modern trajectory of exponential growth to a premodern state of contraction and material decline. The consequences for billions of people should such a scenario play out would be dire.

But even if the leaders of the world's nations were to realise that going from a rapid economic expansion that is dependent upon extraction and consumption to global decline caused by the onset of ecological disasters was not in their interest and that popular economic frameworks have sold them on the false promise of limitless growth. What, if anything, could be done?

The first step is perhaps the hardest. It entails tuning out any economist or economic model advancing the notion that increases in consumption or production that require utilisation of resources are still feasible or desirable. Since all variations of economic growth currently being advocated will lead to ecological collapse within the next 50 years, there is a collective need to start thinking in post-growth terms. The world has more than enough GDP to go around.

The second step is limiting global trade. This can be achieved in two mutually reinforcing ways. One is to shift away from the current trading system based on the United States dollar to a balanced trading system rooted in regional currency blocks that would discourage both excessive imports and exports. The other is to establish a Global Economic Planning Agency that would encourage economic diversification and local production and discourage specialisation and heavy reliance on trade.

The third step would be to impose resource consumption quotas based on per capita income levels. Countries with per capita incomes above 8,500 dollars would be restricted in what they can import by way of energy or what they might themselves produce from fossil fuels. This would compel rich countries to shift to renewable energy. Conversely, poor and middle-income countries would cap their growth once they reached 8,500 dollars per capita GDP.

The fourth step would be to grow through redistribution of wealth and through the promotion of sectors that are not resource-intensive. The redistribution aspect of such a global policy would require both income transfers within all countries from rich to the poor and cancellation of debts, both public and private, domestically and internationally. The growth aspect of this policy would recognise that fields that are not resource-intensive or require minimal material inputs are the most valuable sources of wealth and employment.

The fifth step is to pour resources and effort into the reclamation and restoration of the natural habitat. An initiative, if you will, to terraform the Earth back to health and clean up the mess humans have made. Moving towards the regeneration of nature would also have a positive effect by generating lots of jobs with a negative carbon footprint.

The problem with taking these steps is not that they are not obviously necessary, that there is not sufficient evidence to support the need for drastic action, or even that the logic of avoiding inflicting massive damage on complex systems that might suddenly destabilise once thresholds are crossed is open to question. The problem lies in the realm of politics and administration and the insatiable appetite these have for bad ideas, faulty logic, and selfish decision-making. The relation between intentions and effects represents the governance dimension of our predicament. No matter how wise or benevolent the policy, outcomes depend on the quality of governance and the ability of leaders and states to make wise decisions.

III

Solon and Croesus: Why Humans are Terrible at Making Wise Decisions

> For, to judge aright, one should esteem men because they are generous, not because they have the power to be generous; and, in like manner, should admire those who know how to govern a kingdom, not those who, without knowing how, actually govern one.[1]
> – Machiavelli (Florentine diplomat, writer, and political philosopher, b. 1469, d. 1527)

> Persuading a ruler to adopt the right course is a fatiguing business, but flattery of any emperor is accomplished without the need for real affection.[2]
> – Tacitus (Roman Historian, b. AD 56, d. AD 120)

> But, nowadays, princes and ministers of a disorderly world each on a small scale, appropriates the profits of his own state, and each exercises the burden of his own office, for his private benefit. This is why the states are in a perilous position. For the relation between public and private interests is what determines existence or ruin.[3]
> – Lord Shang (Statesman of the Qin State, c. 390 – 338 BCE)

As the present century unfolds under the intellectual patronage of growth-oriented economists, technological optimists, and corporate apologists, the window of opportunity to save human civilisation from the consequences of ecological collapse is closing. History is often preoccupied with understanding the failures of the past, while philosophers of the subject have built an impressive array of frameworks to help guide those seeking answers. In the year 2200, by which time the present age will probably have ended, post-apocalyptic dystopias would have taken hold of those societies to have survived the onset of Malthusian and Darwinian corrections; a single question will likely consume the historians of that unfortunate time. They would wonder why their ancestors, equipped with modern science and the technical means to save the planet, failed to do so. In their search for answers, they would discover the triumph of hubris, and its companion, nemesis, writ large over the entire course of history and evident in the collapse of earlier civilisations. This being said, pre-modern civilisations were often struck by challenges that were simply beyond their material and organisational capacity to counter. Plagues, famines, barbarian invasions, and natural calamities could strike suddenly and with catastrophic intensity. In the case of modern civilisation, short of an undetected large meteorite striking the Earth, the crises leading to its unravelling have been convincingly predicted for generations.

Herodotus, some 2,500 years ago, as the first critical historian, tried to get to the heart of the human inability to retain rationality in decision-making. The *Histories* written by Herodotus can be read in several equally legitimate ways.[4] The most common way is as a non-linear narrative account of states, cultures, and leaders culminating in the wars between the Persian Empire and the Greek city-states. Another is to take the *Histories* as an authentic, if not always an accurate, account of the civilisation of West Asia, North Africa, and parts of Europe. And then, the *Histories* can be read as a philosophical commentary on the irrationality of power, the heedlessness of the powerful, and innate defects in human nature. This third path through the *Histories* is the most relevant to the present discussion.

Herodotus introduces us to his central insight through the story of Solon of Athens and Croesus of Lydia. Solon, the Athenian statesman, credited with Athens' first constitution, and Croesus, the wealthy ruler of Lydia (now in Turkey), met during the former's travels around 560 BC. Croesus knew about Solon's reputation for learning and wisdom and wanted validation. So, Croesus gave Solon the royal treatment and, after days of generous hospitality, had the Athenian admitted to a royal audience. At this audience, Croesus wanted Solon to tell him who, of all men, was the happiest. Croesus expected that Solon would tell him that he was the happiest of all men. Solon, however, disappointed Croesus by naming Tellus of Athens. In Solon's estimation, Tellus was the happiest of all men as he lived to be 70 in comfort and served his country and was honoured at this death with a public funeral. No man, felt Solon, could aspire to a happier life than one of public service, modest wealth, and popular appreciation.

Croesus was unhappy at this response but was still eager to get Solon's stamp of approval, thus asking Solon to name the second happiest of all men. Upon being disappointed for the second time by Solon's answer, Croesus was livid and demanded to know why the ordinary lives of ordinary men were being described as happier than his own? Solon's response was that until life had ended, it was impossible to render a verdict on it, while such was the cruelty of Providence that it often gave us a taste of joy or success only to take it away. Croesus, blinded by hubris, dismissed Solon. Lydia was soon embroiled in a war with the rising power of Persia, which ended in Persian victory.

Although Herodotus' account of the encounter between Solon and Croesus stretches the timelines of the two lives and is probably apocryphal, it remains useful by providing the *Histories* with a theme. Herodotus uses the mechanism of the voice of reason, giving sound advice whose correctness is proven by the subsequent course of events to demonstrate the toxic effects of power and wealth upon rational decision-making. For Herodotus, human nature is programmed to seek glory and success, but once attained, these acts inhibit rationality and magnify conceit in one's innate superiority. From this hubris flow unwise decisions that lead to frustration, defeat, and, in some cases, collapse. In the *Histories*, everyone succumbs to hubris and invites nemesis making for an exciting story with terrible consequences for the states and societies involved.

From Herodotus, we learn that the greatest public virtue is doing what works to the collective advantage, and the greatest vice is acting out of conceit and ego. At times it is necessary for some to sacrifice themselves for the greater good. Thus, Leonidas leading his 300 Spartans to certain doom at Thermopylae is both heroic and pragmatic as this sacrifice buys time, demoralises the Persians, and helps unite many Greek city-states against the Persian invasion. What makes Leonidas significant is not that his actions are brave but that they are wise, underpinned by *logos* – a logical comprehension of causes and effects. State and decision-making tend to have a directly proportional relationship – the more a state tends towards *logos* in its decision-making, the more likely it is to make wise decisions, and conversely, the lower the level of *logos,* the greater the chances of disaster.

Many of the greatest historians and political thinkers have focused on the vexing contradictions at the heart of all attempts to exercise power with wisdom and effectiveness. The corrupting effects of power deplete the rational and moral faculties needed for its successful exercise. But those who consciously seek power rarely do so out of philosophical foresight or a desire to serve the greater good, assuming they can even comprehend what that is.

The motivation to seek power arises from greed, personal insecurity, social competition, family tradition, identity, ideology, or some combination of these factors. These material, egoistic, or identity-based factors are precisely those associated with hubris. Consequently, those who consciously compete for power are almost invariably intellectually and temperamentally unqualified to wield it wisely. And those who have the temperament and intellect like Solon do not seek it and, should it somehow come their way, wield it for as little time as possible. So, those who cannot exercise power wisely are the most eager to have it, while those who can exercise it wisely do not want to acquire it. This fundamental paradox, rooted in human nature, has operated with equal force across all historical civilisations. It is, therefore, no surprise that all civilisations have wrestled with what Abu'l Fazl, advisor to the Mughal Emperor Akbar (r. 1556-1605), called the problem of the "selfish" ruler.

Abu'l Fazl, in the *Ain-i-Akbari,* divided rulers into two broad categories, i.e. the selfish ruler and the true monarch.[5] The vast majority of rulers fell into the selfish category. Their reigns were characterised by the reckless pursuit of personal gain and pleasure. These rulers confused the trappings of power with the substance needed to govern fairly, wisely, and efficiently. Selfish rulers attracted vicious and incompetent courtiers, for they were incapable of taking good advice. In this manner, the decline of the state became inevitable, along with the ruin of the country. A minority of rulers, who fell into the "true" category, were characterised by their ability to comprehend that statesmanship and governance were the mainsprings of greatness. Decisions by such rulers reflected the overall interests of the state. The less selfishly a ruler behaved, the better would be the quality of administration, the more prosperous society would become, and the longevity of the regime would be ensured.

The Chinese engaged with the problem of the "bad emperor", the Persians wrote "mirrors for princes", the Ottomans crafted a Platonic military-bureaucratic slave elite – the janissaries – to run their empire and advise them, and Ibn Khaldun, the great Arab philosopher of history, wrote profoundly about the structural processes that underpinned the rise and fall of states. The basic blueprint of the great empires forged by the Arabs, Turks, Persians, Mughals, and the Chinese was a monarchical ruler exercising power through hierarchies of civil servants, soldiers, priests, and notables. Despite all the emphasis on enlightened self-interest, princely education, selection of capable servants, and cultivation of a drive to leave an enduring constructive legacy, these continental bureaucratic empires could not resolve the problem of the selfish ruler or ensure the orderly succession of wise monarchs.

While most of the world's successful civilisations were organised as enlightened autocracies, the Western world, with its classical republics, feudal aristocracies, and modern liberal or constitutionalist experiments, took a different route in addressing the paradox identified by Herodotus. While the dominant Eurasian tradition tried to ensure a high quality of autocratic rule mediated through imperial servants, the Western tradition sought to limit the power of any single actor while rendering all actors vulnerable to the law or the collective will.

Athenian democracy, Spartan oligarchy, the Roman Republic, the feudal diffusion of power, the Magna Carta, modern constitutionalism inspired by Montesquieu and the separation of powers, and the pursuit of democracy represent some historically important manifestations of the effort to moderate the effects of power on its wielders. These approaches share a common understanding of the power paradox. First, they all accept that the concentration of too much power in one person or institution is more likely to produce abuses. Second, they regard competition between elites as a good thing that imposes mutual restraint while encouraging better performance so long as the rules of the game are accepted as legitimate. Third, they emphasise institutional continuity through a predictable method of succession. Fourth, the shared expectation is that if the first three points are followed, then the decisions of government will have greater legitimacy within the elite and, where applicable, in society at large. And finally, from this legitimacy will flow a less coercive state wherein authority, being exercised with the consent of powerful sections of society, will be carried into effect more completely.

In practice, societies organised on the republican, aristocratic, corporate, or liberal-constitutionalist pattern extant in the West are plutocracies. A small and incredibly wealthy elite secures political and administrative power through direct and indirect means and ensures that the state serves the selfish interests of the top 0.1 per cent. Historically, such plutocracies have proven far more brittle than autocracies with territorial expansion or great power status, often leading to the rapid erosion of the elite consensus sustaining these state configurations. It is not surprising, therefore, that much of the political thought emerging from the Western experience of relative diffusion of power fixates on the problem of institutional decay arising from the selfish and unwise conduct of elites in such systems. From Aristotle, Plato, and Cicero, to Locke, Voltaire, and Montesquieu, to present-day democratic theorists, the search for a stable and responsive moderate regime continues with only illusive successes due to the inherent limitations of this approach.

The first limitation is that more competition between elites does not produce rulers better able to govern but only rulers better at winning the competition to occupy a limited number of authority positions. Indeed, as Peter Turchin has observed, the over-production of elites can have a destabilising effect on public institutions leading to unhealthy competition and the emergence of counter-elites alienated from the system.[6] The more vicious and intense the competition, the less likely ethical candidates are to compete, and their chances of success would be even lower.

The second constraint on the quality of candidates is the financial cost of political competition. Even in a developed democracy, like the United States, there are few restrictions on candidates taking vast sums of money to run their campaigns from lobbies funding Political Action Committees and then, if they win, helping write legislation for the interests that bankrolled their electoral success.[7] The greater the size of the electorate, the more it will cost in terms of outreach, mobilisation, and media content to get the message out. In more aristocratic or feudal settings, it is still expensive to buy a constituency through the exercise of patronage. And in those cases, frequently found in the developing world, where overt religious or social affiliation causes a constituency to vote for a candidate because of their lineage or spiritual value, monopoly leads to incompetence and self-aggrandisement.[8] Perhaps the most poignant recent instance of the power of money in politics was Senator Marco Rubio of Florida, refusing to rule out taking any more money from the National Rifle Association when asked to do so point-blank by children from his constituency who had survived a school shooting.[9] Rubio is not the exception but the rule. To keep the money rolling, most politicians, even in the West, are literally prepared to allow their constituents and their children to die.[10] Whether that death comes quickly, in the form of a mass shooting, or slowly, in the form of climate change, is a matter of detail.

The third faultline emanates from limited durations in tenures. Such limits are intrinsic to democracy and other constitutional forms of government. After every few years, leaders need to refresh their mandate. Elections can be coordinated so that they all happen at once or staggered, as is the case in the United States, or a mixture of the two, as in India or Pakistan. In theory, periodic elections should make governments more responsive. In actuality, they lead the political class to operate in a permanent campaign mode that consumes most of its energy. To stay in power becomes an end in itself rather than a means to an end or a way to serve the public interest. Depending on how the election cycles play out, divided governments, shaky majorities, or weak coalitions may emerge, all of which reinforce the primacy of survival in politics.

The fourth constraint stems from the vested interests and inertia of the administrative instruments under the command of the political leadership. Such instruments include the personalised power networks associated with the expansion of the Roman Republic, the service nobilities and scribal bureaucracies of pre-modern empires, and modern bureaucratic organisations. The BBC's classic comedy series, *Yes Minister*, and its successor, *Yes Prime Minister*, capture the eternal battle between the "political will" and "administrative wont", painting a remarkably authentic portrait of government as a "loose confederation of warring tribes".[11]

While the characters and situations are fictional, the basic message is solidly based on the historical reality of administrative institutions. That is, the instruments of administration are far from being neutral, and they can effectively frustrate even the most popular government in the pursuit of the most sensible policies. Even the most highly regarded bureaucracies, like the Japanese elite track or French Grand Corps, seek to limit the scope of political action to what they deem to be practical. The opposite approach is for political leaders to have a spoils system (as happens in the United States) and appoint thousands of people presumably loyal to their political vision to key positions. This approach creates fissures within the apparatus and undermines its ability to move at all by privileging loyalty over competence. It also exacerbates the danger of vested interests that bankroll campaigns infiltrating the bureaucracies that exist to regulate them, such as appointing coal lobbyists and climate change deniers to the United States Environmental Protection Agency.[12] The choice then is between a highly autonomous and professional administrative elite basically impervious to political pressure, a compromised bureaucracy staffed through a spoils system or bureaucracies like those of India and Pakistan that manage to combine being formally closed with being substantively politicised and incompetent.

From a broader perspective, autocracies, oligarchies, republics, and democracies contain the seeds of their own destruction. An autocracy depends on the quality of the ruler and the service elite but has no iron clad means to resist a "selfish" ruler. In oligarchies, the interests of the privileged few get conflated with the interests of the state, while competition within the elite can plunge society into chaos. In constitutional republics and democracies, the risk of tyranny through demagoguery or capture of the institutions supposed to represent the public and regulate the powerful by interests averse to both propositions is all too common. In all cases, the barriers that ordinary citizens or subjects need to cross to become decision-makers are immense not only in time and effort but also in terms of finances. Power, as Ibn Khaldun so clearly understood, is tribal, even as the definition of who belongs to our tribe might change.

Another set of critical constraints on our ability to make wise decisions stems from the limitations of our cerebral equipment. People in authority suffer from the same problem of perspective, whereby short-term threats and contemporaneous events grab most of the attention of the general population. Long-term or amorphous threats naturally get shunted to the back of the line. Machiavelli's observation that problems are hard to detect when manageable and easy to detect once they become unmanageable gets to the heart of our inability to act in time to stop great disasters. The other side of this is the amount of distraction that people in authority have to put up with. It helps to think of a state and a society as a series of relationships. The more relationships converge on a single point, the more powerful the occupier of that point turns. So, in manorial feudalism, the lord of the manor occupies the most important point because the serfs, freeholders, and his vassals need the manor to do everything from deciding their disputes to selling their grain and organising civic life.

As Alexis de Tocqueville observed in *The Old Regime and the Revolution*, the French Revolution became possible not because feudalism was strong in France but because between 1600 and 1789, an increasingly absolutist state instrumented through a royal bureaucracy and the army had created parallel and, ultimately, more powerful networks, dependent upon key officials (especially the intendants).[13] These royal servants were eventually replaced by a modern bureaucracy headed at the local level by prefects – a system that is still contemporaneous in France. The dilemma is that without the concentration of power, effective governance is impossible. But that same concentration means that key officials, ministers, and top executives are overwhelmed by information and distractions. They are also subjected to pressure by lobbies and vested interests, some of which were or are critical to their coming into power or staying there. Even if the political leadership wants to do the right thing and is fully seized of the importance of a particular policy, the resistance it will face is considerable. Should the leadership somehow tune out the noise and manage external pressures and bureaucratic inertia, it might still fail to act wisely because of the power of identity. All power is social and requires motivating people to follow the leader or motivating some people to coerce others to follow the leader. In premodern times a combination of kinship and religious belief provided the glue that held regimes together. In modern times, notions of ethnicity, nationhood, or utopian ideologies - civil religions, as Michael Burleigh calls them - produce the same effect.[14] How a state or community identifies itself places limits on what is politically possible.

Some cultures, like those of the United States, are so enamoured with the idea of free enterprise and individualism associated with capitalism that they just cannot accept that a stationary state or equilibrium is necessary or possible.[15] Similarly, Japan's elite mandarins and their political allies are so emotionally invested in the idea of Japan as a homogenous and harmonious society that they can only, with great difficulty, wrap their heads around the need to open their society to immigration to offset demographic trends such as greying of the population and insufficient numbers in the workforce.[16] In Europe, national identities that were supposed to have been rendered redundant by the European project and the shared European values that are embodied by the European Union (EU) are reasserting themselves in spite of the tragic history of the 1900s.[17]

In a contest between our imagined identities and real-world, long-term interests, the former frequently trump the latter. The history of governance furnishes little basis for optimism. Human nature is almost invariably tribal, selfish, and prone to collective delusions that have, with agonising regularity, caused us to deny the humanity of others. For all the political wisdom and administrative experience of the imperial civilisations and bureaucratic states of Eurasia, the problem of the selfish ruler remains intractable. For all the redemptive potential and inspiring rhetoric of its classical and modern political philosophies, Western societies are constitutional plutocracies where the capture of institutional power by an assortment of vested interests that do not have the public good at heart is the norm. Between our inherent weakness and the damage accumulated over time, there appears to be no satisfactory answer to the problem of sustaining the wise and efficient exercise of power. These deficiencies might have been tolerable had human social and political development proceeded at about the same pace as technological advancement and economic growth. For the past 500 years, however, the pace of material change has far exceeded the evolution of cultures of power, group mentality, and our ability to understand in a relatable manner the behaviour of the complex systems that sustain the Earth. With resources running low and consumption and population continuing to rise rapidly, the time to take countermeasures to save the planet has practically run out. As the global environmental emergency asserts itself and becomes obvious, the costs of doing anything about it escalate dramatically. Having not taken action when the problem was manageable, the costs of taking effective action today have become prohibitive. Critical tipping points to avert a planetary crisis, be they related to biodiversity loss, habitat loss, toxicity, or global warming, have either been crossed or are so close that limiting the damage is all we can reasonably hope to do. Many of our thinkers and practically all of our leaders have, like Croesus, refused to listen to Solon's admonishment. Modern civilisation may well become that brief glimpse of happiness that is cruelly overshadowed by nemesis rooted in our hubris.

In 1972, a report titled *The Limits to Growth* was published as part of the Club of Rome's project on the future of the world.[18] The authors were researchers in their mid-20s. The report was meant to serve as a timely warning to the world's leaders that exponential material growth was unsustainable on a planet with finite resources. Even the most optimistic projection indicated that the Earth's resources would run out within 100 years. By 2100, or perhaps sooner, the Earth would be a wasteland unable to support energy-intensive human civilisation and horrific Malthusian and natural corrections would start ravaging humanity by 2050. The basic message that the authors wanted to convey was that the world's governments, businesses and thinkers needed to work in concert to bring the global economy into equilibrium with the Earth's carrying capacity. Such equilibrium would not end economic growth but decouple it from gross increases in material consumption and production.

The case made by *The Limits to Growth* was solid and has been strengthened by the passage of time as its concerns are now widely shared by environmentalists and governments. The report made a huge splash in the public domain and was widely reviewed and commented upon. It angered economists, heartened environmentalists, and engaged political leaders. However, the policy impact of the report was negligible. In theory, public officials, when they encounter a superior argument about policy, should change their minds. This should be all the more so in instances where national, and collective survival is at stake. There were five major causes for the triumph of Croesus's hubris over Solon's *logos* in this specific instance. The first reason why the argument advanced by *The Limits to Growth* proved unviable was that it ran counter to the dominant themes of modern political and economic discourse, which made the attainment of material prosperity and a high standard of living the fundamental goal of governance. The report warned that global industrialisation to Western levels was ecologically ruinous and would destroy the planet. For the political leaderships of developing countries, many of whom were ravaged by centuries of brutal colonial exploitation by Western powers, the idea that they cannot catch up to the West because that will destroy the planet is deeply hurtful and unacceptable. The leaders of India or China cannot tell their people, "Sorry, but in order to save the Earth, we will have to cap our economic growth and consumption at a level of 10-20 per cent of the West, which is, incidentally, partly responsible for our poverty through its colonial exploitation".

For the leaders of rich countries, *The Limits to Growth* hypothesis, if accepted, would require imposing restrictions on further increases in consumption and following a redistributive agenda that would hurt the politically significant top one per cent of their societies. In fact, the Western world embraced the neoclassical or neoliberal mantra of free markets and the celebration of the resulting inequality in the late-1970s and early-1980s. They entrenched neoliberal ideas in institutions like the IMF and the World Bank. It makes little difference to the average American household if Bill Gates or Jeff Bezos earn extra billions (that get added to GDP and overall growth). The three richest Americans have more wealth than the bottom 60 per cent of American households.[19] Besides, if every country had the per capita consumption of China, then the Earth could sustain seven billion people. But at the United States' levels of consumption, three or four planet earths would be needed.[20] The Chinese, however, are determined to rise to developed country status, while no American government could seriously cut per capita consumption by 80 per cent. The political will to achieve ecological equilibrium is just not there and cannot be there, as democracies cannot deliberately make their people poorer, while enlightened autocracies derive their legitimacy from economic growth. Even today, the IMF considers the world economy to be in recession if it grows less than three per cent a year, which is to say that the IMF believes that unless global GDP doubles every 24 years, there is insufficient growth.[21]

The second impediment to the acceptance of *The Limits to Growth* hypothesis was and still is administrative. Let us say that the world's leaders accept that taking effective action to achieve equilibrium is necessary. Implementation will fall to the civil service elites and the bureaucracies under their command. The targets of such policies will be everybody, from large corporations to individual citizens. Many of the close relationships that bureaucracies have with important segments of society will be disrupted. The interests of commerce and industry will, in particular, be adversely affected by policies stringent enough to actually save the planet in the time we have left. Consequently, there will be fierce pushback.

In democracies, civil society will protest and resist the intrusion of the state. Corporations and their lobbyists will kick up a storm. The resistance will assume legal and popular forms. Delays will be inevitable and widespread, rewards will appear remote, and costs will be immediate. Enlightened autocracies would, in principle, have an advantage in that legal opposition would not be an issue, nor would civil society. The problem would arise from the risk of popular rebellion driven by restrictions on standards of living. Implementation of a strict environmentalist agenda would also disrupt relationships within the state apparatus and between the regime and its wealthiest subjects. In democracies and autocracies with effective administrations, there is a chance that steps taken to achieve equilibrium will be enforced. But the vast majority of states, whether democratic or autocratic, do not have the ability to establish effective environmental administrations. Countries like India and Pakistan cannot manage garbage collection or basic sanitation in their capitals. To expect that they can pursue a complicated set of policies aimed at achieving environmental and socioeconomic equilibrium is not realistic.

The third impediment arises from the structure of globalisation and the market economy. Shifting to greener local production and limiting world trade will disrupt existing supply and demand chains. Those who profit from globalised trade in commodities, especially export-oriented economies like Germany and China, will find the adjustment painful. Germany, the poster child for an environmentally responsible industrialised state, is a case in point. Since the mid-1990s, Germany has spent nearly 600 billion dollars on converting its economy to renewable sources of energy. In absolute terms, Germany has achieved cuts in carbon emissions but missed nearly all of its 2020 targets by a wide margin.[22] The reductions that have been achieved were more than offset by increasing emissions in other countries. The tremendous growth in the fortunes of the top 0.1 per cent since 1975 means that Davos men and women are better funded than ever before and might well now constitute a global imperial elite that will resist any serious effort to impose the restrictions needed to de-globalise trade in commodities, tax the very rich, and pay for a rapid transition to greener economies.

Saving the Earth will necessitate dealing with the billionaires in a Bolshevik manner because they are the ultimate enemies of the planet and the billions of underprivileged that inhabit it. The interface, however, between governments, plutocrats, and administrations is so strong that breaking it up through the normal processes of politics is no longer possible within the remaining time. Even mild proposals like increasing marginal tax rates on the highest incomes, cracking down on offshore accounts, or imposing carbon taxes meet with furious and effective opposition from the privileged few who stand to lose from them.[23]

The fourth impediment arises from the lag between implementation and effect. No one can be entirely sure how quickly the Earth's ecology will recover even if maximal pro-equilibrium proposals are set in place in the 2020s. It may not be possible to reverse the damage within a timeframe relevant to civilisation. Even in the most environmentally conscious country, the lags are immense and outcomes difficult to predict. Turning around 200 countries, even if they are all committed, will take time, and progress will be uneven. The uncertainty of success in achieving equilibrium in time encourages state elites to pay lip service to the needs of the environment while positioning themselves to acquire the best possible control over the Earth's remaining resources. This cynical social Darwinism explains China's drive to acquire control over African mineral wealth,[24] key shipping lanes,[25] and its One Belt One Road initiative.[26] The deaths of millions of less wealthy Asians, Africans, and Latin Americans, from the effects of a four degrees Celsius temperature increase by the end of this century, while tragic, are inevitable from a *realpolitik* perspective.

The fifth impediment arises from the slow pace of philosophical change. Academia and the broader intelligentsia are the products of structures that have been at the leading edge of globalisation and sustained pro-growth economic theories and technological optimism. Things are changing, but the pace of innovation and the opening up of new avenues of consumption means that most of our thinkers are not engaged with the mortal threat posed by the collapse of the Earth's ecology. One of the major contributors to *The Limits to Growth*, Dennis L. Meadows, was constrained to admit in 2012 that while he was pleased that the questions posed by that study were being seriously considered 40 years after its release, he no longer felt we could stop the economic doomsday machine in time.[27] The leisurely pace at which new ideas are circulated and tested and accepted or rejected by academia and the press mean that even the best ideas take an awfully long time to gain traction. Since universities provide the human resource for businesses, corporations, state services, and political parties, generations can be blinded by unsound ideas such as limitless economic growth and pursue policies based on what they have learned.

Notwithstanding our admiration for wise statesmen like Solon, it is unwise, like Croesus, that have exercised power for most of our history. Herodotus teaches us that nemesis awaits those who have succumbed to hubris leading to the rise and fall of empires and states. The basic constraints on wise decision-making, being rooted in human nature, cut across history. The tragedy that is presently unfolding is that if the spirit of Croesus prevails again, then the story of modern human civilisation will end within a few generations.

IV

The Pangloss Effect: Why Optimism is Lethal

Men from shortsightedness frequently seek their own advantage in what is harmful to them: how much the more must they err in regard to others.[1]
– Akbar the Great (Mughal Emperor, r. 1556-1605)

Never has an expedition against them been more certain of success...[2]
– Napoleon Bonaparte (French Emperor, r. 1804-1815, on the prospect of war with the Russian Empire)

Optimism – or the idea that our inherent ability to overcome problems is greater than the chance our problems overcome us – is perhaps the most prevalent and indefatigable of all imaginative viruses to infect humans. It lies at the root of the greatest disasters in history and has seriously compromised humanity's response to the global ecological catastrophe. Optimists are generally willing to give human beings the benefit of the doubt or simply invent the doubt necessary to continue giving themselves and others like them a pass. The most diehard of this lot, no matter how bad things get, will remain true to the notion advanced by Professor Pangloss in Voltaire's *Candide* that we live "in the best of all possible worlds". What makes Pangloss remarkable is his ability to explain away all the terrible things that happen to Candide (the hero) as being somehow for the best. The more disasters befall Candide; the more elaborate Pangloss becomes in his rationalisations.[3]

The sources of our optimism are many, but three, in particular, merit mention. The first of these is rooted in biology and the well-attested inability of our animal brains to react to difficulties unless they are immediate. Over millions of years, humans evolved to excel at responding to immediate dangers with a range of xenophobic and cooperative responses hardwired into them. Just think of how your mind focuses on any strange sound or how tribal we are in our social life with multiple layers of in-groups and out-groups requiring "us" to work together against "them". At the same time, absent an immediate threat, humans focus on what is convenient or pleasing and ignore all else.

The second is rooted in our imagination and its effects on our ability to understand the causes of phenomena around us. As the exercise of reason requires effort and often produces unpleasant effects, human beings are vulnerable to any assertion of certainty. Historically, the easiest way to be sure about things is to imagine an explanation or attribute causes to supernatural forces and repeat it endlessly. According to the 18th century Italian philosopher Giambattista Vico, the exercise of this imaginative faculty was an important binding force in early civilisations. The xenophobic and cooperative tendencies rooted in our biology found expression in what Vico called "poetic wisdom",[4] whereby cooperation on a large scale to placate or fight against the supernatural forces responsible for natural processes that often harmed humans emerged. It also meant that humans who believed in a different set of deities could be identified as outsiders. But the greatest asset of poetic wisdom was its infinite elasticity in explaining human suffering and the many calamities that afflicted people at the individual and collective levels. Religion, ideology, popular superstitions, *dharma*, *karma*, modern wellness tropes, and a variety of other ideas brilliantly dissected by Francis Wheen in *How Mumbo Jumbo Conquered the World* help people stay hopeful.[5] Statements that celebrate as a "miracle" the survival of one person out of scores or hundreds in an accident or rags-to-riches stories are classical instances of such thinking.

The third source of optimism is self-centeredness. Over the past three hundred years, as traditional ideas have become less appealing, materialism and consumerism have provided secular means of helping us stay hopeful. Global elites are particularly fierce advocates of material optimism, while those who have succeeded enough in terms of conventional bourgeois standards also strongly identify with this type of thinking. For the globalised classes, their privileges and prosperity encourage them to rationalise it as being a desirable outcome for all with the promise held out that everyone could have a Swiss standard of living.[6] So, while the world's richest 75 million people contribute as much to global warming as the poorest 3.75 billion,[7] the metropolitan optimist remains supremely confident in the ability of humans to turn the tables on the impending global catastrophe. In this way, without having to change our ravenous behaviour, we will find a miraculous solution to our predicament, and this will remain, now and forever, the best of all possible worlds. Our optimism is built on the solid foundations of biology, ideology, and self-absorption.

It is no surprise that optimistic thinking has produced disastrous consequences throughout history. One does not have to go very far back to find instances of optimism leading to catastrophic miscalculations. The 20th century began with the drift to the First World War – a conflict that claimed 20 million lives directly[8] and at least an additional 20-30 million lives indirectly.[9] Amongst the most critical causes of the conflict was the idea that war would be won swiftly and cheaply, enabling an advantageous reset of the global pecking order. Every great power that entered the war was convinced that victory was one campaign away. Had the rulers of Europe been pessimists and sceptics, they would have been less likely to fall prey to militarist and nationalist fantasies. In spite of the enormous trauma endured by the participants in the First World War, most retained a resolutely optimistic outlook on the future.

This optimism was the result of revolutions in Russia, Italy, and Germany which brought to power left-wing and right-wing utopians.[10] In United States, the return of the country to isolationism represented the triumph of the hope that the world would sort itself out and that even if it did not, the great oceans would protect the American homeland.[11] In Britain and France, the nominal victors of the First World War, a pacifist fantasy took hold of public discourse – one that led to the appeasement of fascism while it was militarily weak. This pacifism also led to the demoralising concessions once it became apparent that Germany had rearmed and was ready for a rematch. In Japan, the decline of European colonial empires and the return of the United States to isolation led to the articulation of an imperial vision for Asia, in which China would become Japan's India, and the rest of the continent would thrive under Japanese tutelage. The bill for these various shades of optimistic thinking came due in the form of a global conflict that dwarfed the First World

War and raged in China from 1931 to 1945 and in the rest of the world from 1939 to 1945, killing 60-70 million,[12] and injuring or displacing many times that number. The trouble is that until the Japanese bombs fell on Pearl Harbor, most Americans genuinely believed that they could wait out the World War. The appeasement governments of 1930s France and Britain did what their people thought was best. In spite of credible evidence pouring in that Hitler had zero interest in peace and was not a rational actor, the French and British (and later the Soviets) chose a policy of hope over reality. Hitler and many in his circle were convinced that they stood at the threshold of a Thousand Year Reich to establish the German master race as the dominant world power. Lenin and his successors were equally firm in their belief that the communist utopia they were building in the Soviet Union would carry the world with it and that history was on their side. The Japanese, debilitated by overdoses of nationalism and imperial ambition, also believed that they were destined to hold the future of half of humanity in their hands. While optimism fueled by ideological or popular conviction led to the greatest disasters of the first half of the 20th century, the relative peace that descended on the world post-1945 led to the emergence of an even more lethal variant of optimism.

After 1945, elites and peoples of all ideologies and at all developmental levels embraced materialistic optimism. This is the idea that human life can only get better through the application of technology and economic growth. Soviet oligarchs, Maoist tyrants, social democrats, Keynesian economists, Third World nationalists, medieval fossil fuel monarchies, and neoliberal shock therapists shared the unshakeable belief that getting rich was, and is, glorious. Their disagreement was on the best way to organise a society to achieve that end. Should societies be forced to undergo a Maoist "Great Leap Forward", or is it better to maintain a high investment-to-GDP ratio for a few decades, or is state ownership the key, or should the decisions be left to the "free" market, were the debates that raged within and between groups of growth cultists. But what was never really questioned was the logic of infinite growth. The result was that since 1945 all of the nations stopped waging the kind of total wars that had characterised the first half of the 20th century. Alternatively, they decided to wage total war upon our planet in pursuit of the elixir of infinite growth and prosperity. With extraordinary and increasing intensity, all other life on Earth was subjected to an industrialised massacre. Ecology and climate-altering amounts of chemicals and compounds were poured into the land, sea, and air to make way for a better life for more humans. As evidence mounted in the 1960s, 1970s, and 1980s that the war on nature would lead to the collapse of the environmental and biological systems humans needed for their survival, our optimistic minds either refused to contemplate that dreadful probability or pinned hopes on technology delivering a solution.[13] Like the millions of people who thought the Nazis ought to be appeased, successive generations after 1945 thought that we would somehow muddle through and the worst-case scenarios would not materialise. Even when the awareness was there, the willingness to move quickly enough to avert catastrophe was insufficient.

At present, as we head into the third decade of what may be the final century for humans, the collapse of biodiversity is threatening to disrupt the agricultural cycle, global warming is rendering much of the current inhabited zone uninhabitable, and for every extinction rebellion activist, there are far more people swayed by populism, greed, and identity politics. One important factor that works to enhance the Pangloss effect is that since the 1970s, life has gotten better for the top 1-10 per cent of nearly every country's population. What this means is that those people with the greatest agency and best opportunities have experienced a world that is getting better for them. Naturally, they do not want this trend reversed even when they understand, at an intellectual level, the terrible costs it has imposed on the 80 per cent of the world's population that has gotten relatively poorer since 1975[14] or the 60 per cent that does not earn enough (about seven to eight dollars a day) to feed and clothe itself adequately, or around 93 per cent that do not have a college or university degree.[15] The improvements that have taken place in reducing infant and maternal mortality or improving access to healthcare or education have almost nothing to do with the operation of the global economy and nearly everything to do with the ability of individual states to provide services and subsidise their citizens – both activities being constantly threatened by the austerity axe wielded by neoliberals and their apologists ensconced in international financial institutions and world markets. In spite of having achieved sufficient world GDP per capita in 2000 (8,500 dollars) to provide every person with a dignified life without exceeding the natural carrying capacity of the world, the top 1-10 per cent have insisted on enriching themselves and outsourcing the costs of their plunder.[16] For instance, a country like Pakistan, which contributes a mere 0.8 per cent of the world's GHG emissions, is nonetheless ranked as the eighth most vulnerable to the effects of global warming.[17] Or we can take India that barely has 22 cars per 1,000 people compared to over 800 per 1,000 in the United States,[18] which is facing prolonged heat waves and disruption of its agricultural cycle due, in part, to climate change.[19]

This brings us to the darker, hubristic side of the Pangloss effect as it relates to the global elites. For many in the West, the sense is that even if a few billion peasants and slum dwellers in the Global South perish as a result of environmental collapse, the global metropolis will be able to employ its accumulated wealth and technology to continue to thrive behind hard borders. They are prepared to make concessions to the public conscience, such as declaring environmental emergencies or promising to achieve net-zero GHG emissions by 2050,[20] or, as the Shell CEO recently advised, encouraging people to eat seasonally.[21] But while these apparent victories are handed out to the environmental lobby, the United Kingdom, for instance, has cut subsidies for solar power[22] while British Petroleum continues to send out rigs to drill for oil and gas.[23] Within developing countries, the spike in global inequality has benefited elites tremendously, and there is widespread contempt for the poor reinforced by a variety of caste, communal, and tribal identities. The "Globish" elite of the developing world feels closer to its metropolitan counterparts when it comes to seeing the great mass of the Asian, African, and Latin American poor as surplus humans and the remaining resources of their homelands as means to get even richer often in cahoots with international capital. Third world globalists might actually live better than their first world equivalents, with the former living in air-conditioned comfort in gated communities with a large underclass to provide them with lots of domestic help. Consequently, they are just as vulnerable to the delusion that when environmental collapse strikes, it will not affect them or think that if things get really bad, they can flee to the West. Unwilling to change their behaviour or even limit their enrichment, metropolitan and peripheral globalist elites have great faith in the human ability to find a technical solution to the multifaceted environmental crisis. Perhaps there will soon be plastic-eating microbes that will clean up our land and oceans; a massive cloning program to restore global biodiversity; carbon-capture technology to reverse global warming; a new global breadbasket will emerge in Siberia and the Arctic to keep humanity fed; AI will save the day by making everything more efficient; humans will become an interplanetary species. Of course, even a little logical thinking about any of these will reveal that they are untenable. Releasing vast quantities of plastic-eating microbes into our environment might well help contain waste, but the evolutionary trajectory of these organisms will be rapid and unpredictable. More importantly, the plastic industry is closely tied to the fossil fuel industry, and without ending mass consumption of plastics, the problem will likely get worse. As for cloning, yes, it would make sense to save species this way, but for one basic biological problem. Clones would lack genetic diversity and be highly vulnerable to being wiped out by disease. Also, the rate at which plant and animal life are going extinct is so rapid that we have already lost hundreds of thousands of species. It is not clear whether enough could be saved to restore the ecosystem to health.

Carbon capture is a pipe dream because the number of resources and energy it would take to reduce GHGs in the atmosphere and have negative emissions large enough to reverse global warming trends would be self-defeating. It is also probably too late as vital tipping points have been crossed. For instance, the extent of Arctic summer ice melt is expected to reach by 2035, levels not anticipated till 2090.[24] The thawing of Siberia and the Arctic/Antarctic might well produce a new breadbasket, but if the same intensive farming techniques are applied, the soil will degrade within a few decades. There are also bacteria and viruses lurking in the melt against which humans have no immunity.[25] Sending large numbers of people to settle in these regions is probably not the best idea,[26] while the scramble for Arctic territory is likely to produce great power conflict.[27] For all our space cadets, there is the unfortunate fact that the Earth is now surrounded by debris and that the carbon cost of spaceflight is so great that sending large numbers to other worlds is not feasible. Even if large numbers could be sent, what exactly would they do on the Moon or on Mars (the two likeliest destinations) that might help save humanity back on Earth? Terraforming is possible (over centuries), at least in the case of Mars, but it would require massive investment from a dying Earth. And would it not make more sense to do what was needed to save the one planet in our solar system where the air is breathable than squandering resources on trying to make another place more like Earth?

But the Pangloss effect is so powerful that nothing can deter the optimist from believing that the future is only going to be better. Optimists cannot seriously contemplate any reality in which their lives and convenience are no longer sustainable, nor can they accept that defeat is inevitable unless we put aside our Pangloss lenses. Optimists, in practice, would rather condemn their children and the planet to an agonising demise while retaining the cheerful disposition made possible by their inability to study the abyss that lies before us. Being unable to comprehend reality, optimists are less likely to actually do what is needed to survive. Modern optimists are in such complete thrall to the delusion of human power that they have almost universally succumbed to the power of human delusion. To save the planet and, incidentally, ourselves, humans, especially the rich and clever ones, need to stop being optimistic and embrace realism, scepticism, and pessimism. Pessimism and its cousins — realism and scepticism — are often wrongly understood as negativism or cynicism. Many people who would consider themselves optimists, like economists who adhere to Nordhaus's absurd analysis of the GDP impact of climate change, are in functional terms negative and cynical.[28] This is so because they sell people a placebo and set everybody up for catastrophic failure. In contrast, a pessimist would argue that we ought to comprehend our trajectory logically. If that analysis leads us to conclude that the trajectory is terminal, then realistically, we have two options. The first is to try to avert the outcome, and the other is to find a way to survive it if it is unavoidable. Let's illustrate this approach with some examples from history.

During the 1930s, fascism was ascendant, and after the advent of Nazi rule in Germany, it appeared that a new and irresistible force in world affairs was emerging. The overwhelming majority of the British and French people wanted peace, and their political leaders shared this pious hope. Hitler, as communicated by the French and British ambassadors to Berlin, was not interested in peace. He wanted war and was fanatically committed to Nazi ideology. In pursuit of ideological objectives, Hitler was prepared to show tactical flexibility, but the outcomes he sought were predetermined. While governments in the United Kingdom and France tried to do business with Hitler, Winston Churchill, an out of favour old-timer, repeatedly warned that the Nazis were dead serious about their insane ideology and that they were not seeking accommodation but an advantageous strategic position from which to annihilate all opposition to their millennial utopian vision.[29] From Churchill's perspective, every concession to Nazi Germany merely delayed an inevitable conflict to a point in the future where the Allies would be relatively weaker.

Churchill was being pessimistic. He desperately wanted to save his country from a calamitous war with Nazi Germany and felt that this required reacting harshly to Hitler's foreign policy while the Allies still held the military advantage. For nearly six years, Churchill opposed public opinion, defied his party's leadership, and incurred the wrath of the great and the good. By the time the rest of his country had woken up to the reality of a Nazi Empire, the war had begun on less favourable terms. Elevated in the midst of this crisis to the premiership, Churchill proved to be a ruthless warlord utterly committed to the destruction of Nazi Germany. Churchill's essential strategic insight was that Hitler was ideologically driven and would be propelled by his worldview to relentlessly expand the conflict to hasten the achievement of the Nazi millennium. To his people, Churchill's message was stark. Even if the United Kingdom fell to the Nazis, the war would continue because a world dominated by Nazism was not one worth living in. In other words, by the end of May 1940, Churchill resolved to risk the destruction of his homeland (even though the Nazis were prepared to cut a deal) in order to defeat a threat that, if allowed to prevail, would have turned the world into a nightmarish racial dystopia. It is to this heroic pessimism, more than anything else, that Churchill owes his place in history.

Two older instances of pessimism inducing rational thinking are of Metternich and Bismarck. The former wrestled with the old problem of Central Europe (i.e. Germany being either too weak or too strong for the peace of Europe) and devised the German Confederation – a union of Germanic principalities strong enough to deter attack but sufficiently decentralised to avoid being tempted into aggression.[30] After the rise of German nationalism proved too much for the loose structure of the Confederation to bear, Prussia, under Bismarck, ejected Austria from the organisation and united the rest of Germany into a single state.

Once this unification was achieved, Bismarck changed tack and declared that Germany was content with the new map of Europe. He proceeded to reconcile Austria, befriend Russia, keep Britain neutral, and ensure France had no major allies with which to encircle the new Central European giant. For Bismarck, an overly aggressive foreign policy would lead to the rapid encirclement of Germany and risk plunging it into a war on multiple fronts. After Bismarck's exit in 1890, a new generation of optimistic German leaders who were supremely confident in their nation's newfound success abandoned the policy of restraint and gradual accumulation of strength through development and embarked upon a global policy aimed at securing their country's place amongst the three global empires (Britain, France, and Russia).

The result was as Bismarck feared. By 1894, France and Russia became allies, followed a decade later by France and Britain, and by 1907, Germany had succeeded in driving all three empires into an anti-German alliance. In some respects, the world is confronting a situation similar to a century ago, with China as the emerging superpower. Under Deng Xiaoping, Jiang Zemin, and Hu Jintao, China focused on its internal development and became a development success story by rejecting neoliberal ideas and focusing on using its state-regulated economy to gain a competitive advantage over Western rivals while investing heavily in improving the lives of its people through governance and welfare spending and eschewing foreign entanglements. Since 2013, however, China has been headed in a more assertive direction and threatening the United States' hegemony in East Asia. This is in part a consequence of greater optimism and confidence arising from unprecedented material prosperity and rising nationalistic sentiment. China's current premier, Xi Jinping, is breaking with Deng Xiaoping's institutional legacy by doing away with term limits, building a cult of personality, and elevating his thought as part of the constitution.

What these and many other instances, such as Napoleon's invasion of Russia, can teach us is that wise leaders try to grasp reality while unwise ones disregard it, often with catastrophic consequences. The trouble is that optimistic rulers, who are normally incapable of wise decision-making, resonate better with people who, in turn, are basically guided by regard for their own convenience. It was perhaps for this reason that Voltaire, a great advocate of the Enlightenment and a leader of the forces of the empire of reason against traditionalism and conventional mindlessness, felt deeply pessimistic in concluding his universal history: "As nature has placed in the heart of man interest, pride, and all the passions, it is no wonder that during a period of about six centuries, we meet with almost a continual succession of crimes and disasters. If we go back to earlier ages, we shall find them no better. Custom has ordered it so that evil has everywhere operated in a different manner."[31] In other words, Pangloss nearly always wins, and the real interests of humanity nearly always lose. This is worth bearing in mind as we examine the geopolitics of a post-apocalyptic world in the next essay.

V

The Geopolitics of Climate Apocalypse

> Power is of three kinds; so is the success resulting from its use. Intellectual strength provides the power of [good] counsel; a prosperous treasury and a strong army provide physical power and valour is the basis for [morale and] energetic action. The success resulting from each one is, correspondingly, intellectual, physical, and [psychological].[1]
> – Kautilya (Philosopher, premier of the Mauryan Empire, c. 300 BC)

Historians often emphasise the role of geography and the environment in shaping human societies. It is no accident that civilisation first arose on the banks of large rivers that existed in close proximity to grassy plains, shrubland, and grazing animals. It is also no surprise that Eurasia and North Africa, with a dominant East-West axis, allowed for swifter diffusion of knowledge than the Americas or Sub-Saharan Africa with their dominant North-South axis. It is possible to stay for longer in the same climatic zone, moving from east to west, while going north or south, environmental conditions change more rapidly. There is also little doubt that bigger and more geographically concentrated populations allowed for more specialists, complex organisations, and elite capture of resources that were only made possible by favourable starting conditions. The ability to better modify the environment to suit humans is also a product of relatively stable geography and ecology susceptible to manipulation. From Ibn Khaldun to Montesquieu[2] and from Fernand Braudel[3] to Jared Diamond,[4] the philosophers of history have maintained with considerable persuasiveness that geographic and environmental factors constituted objective conditions against which societies had to struggle for survival and mastery. To Braudel, the *longue durée,*[5] or time in relation to deep structures, like geography and environment, moved so slowly that it was typically unnoticeable.

Generally, social scientific models subscribed to the idea that geography and environment were stable factors. With honourable exceptions, economists generally assumed that nature would continue to supply the resources needed for growth. Historians and political scientists often observed that ignoring geography and environment proved to be a recipe for military and foreign policy disasters, as evidenced, most recently, by United States military interventions in Vietnam, Afghanistan, and Iraq.[6] Anthropologists and sociologists, through field research, meticulously examined the adaptations made by individuals and groups to their environments.[7] While leaders, soldiers, and diplomats, schooled on these ideas, almost invariably assumed that nature, while open to being exploited and manipulated, constituted the grand chessboard upon which human agency and competition would play out indefinitely. Unfortunately for all remaining life on the planet, human ingenuity, enterprise, and demographic overreach have altered the ecology of the planet to such an extent that those presently alive are, in all probability, the last people to live amidst conditions of environmental stability.[8] The warming of the planet is ushering in a new phase of *Anthropocene* geopolitics that will require leaders to rethink the fundamentals of how they comprehend the world.[9] The climate apocalypse will have enormous consequences for international relations and alter the ways in which states interact.

For most of history, the only way for a society to increase its resources was through horizontal expansion. This was achieved through inland conquest, migration, and establishing colonies overseas.[10] This all-embracing but straightforward fact of history meant that from 4000 BC to AD 1950, a not-so-inconsiderable period, the most successful type of state was the empire. Imperial states were simply asymmetrical power relations in which one group of people dominated or co-opted many other groups of people, with the former drawing resources and labour from the latter to build military might and acquire more land.

This expansion and exploitation process would continue until one empire bumped into another empire (balance of power), ran into an insurmountable natural obstacle (like the Himalayas), lost its internal balance and collapsed into anarchy (political and administrative decline), or faced an overwhelming natural calamity (desiccation, plague, prolonged change in rainfall patterns, etc.).[11] There were alternatives to empire, such as city-states, chiefdoms, or decentralised feudal arrangements (such as those that emerged in Europe after the Roman collapse).[12] But such entities were perennially at risk of being absorbed by empires, while those that became successful and thrived evolved into imperial states. Whatever their provenance, empires produced a metropolitan effect whereby resources, skills, and workers were concentrated in an imperial centre and the hands of a numerically small ruling elite.

After having endured unapologetically for nearly 6,000 years, the imperial model of political order apparently stood discredited. The overseas colonial empires of Europe became nominally independent nation-states. The German, Italian, and Japanese fascist imperial projects lay in ruins. Following the Second World War, the United States and the Soviet Union agreed that henceforth international relations would be conducted under the diplomatic pretence of sovereign equality. Empires would have to be informal and outwardly respectful of the sentiments of the less equal peoples under American or Soviet tutelage. More importantly, the old horizontal model of imperial resource expansion was deemed *passé* in light of the boundless potential for growth and development made possible by technology, trade, and investment in human resources. After 1990, with the Soviet model falling apart, it seemed as if the American version of pro-growth, free-market capitalism would prevail, and everyone would get rich. That, of course, did not happen. What happened was that in pursuit of more economic growth, the Earth's habitability has been compromised, natural resources are depleted, and biodiversity is collapsing.[13] As these constraints assert themselves with growing vigour in the decades ahead, the horizontal expansion will reemerge as the principal means for one society to gain a greater share, or just maintain its existing share, of dwindling resources.

In a neo-Malthusian world, classical imperialism, severe identity polarisation, hard borders, and violent great power competition will return with a vengeance, while the fragile edifice of humanitarianism, internationalism and the veneer of sovereign equality-based diplomacy in all likelihood evaporate.[14] As nations fight each other for resources, especially water and arable land, any increase in resources for one party will have to come from diminishing the resources available to others. Barbarically enforced autarchy on the economic front, militarism on the external front, and autocracy at the political level represent the likely contours of human civilisation amidst climate apocalypse. The return of colonial empires, the extermination of "lesser" peoples, and extreme patriarchy, reinforced by dystopian levels of internal inequality, are not, however, scenarios that global institutions and mainstream thinkers are contemplating. Indeed, the IMF is still pushing for three per cent a year global GDP growth, business as usual dominates the politics and decision-making of all major powers, and most of the developing world is sleepwalking towards the abyss. If history is any guide, the stress on global systems and ecology will accumulate till critical tipping points are crossed. Once enough thresholds have been crossed, the speed of climate change will accelerate to revolutionary levels.

The crisis of resource depletion is severe, but innovation and recycling, as well as forced cuts to consumption, might well be able to mitigate its effects – at least in countries with reasonably effective governance. What will prove fatal for many countries will be the crisis of habitability caused by global warming.[15] In the past, even minor fluctuations in the planet's climate triggered mass migrations and conflicts. For instance, the Indus Valley Civilisation probably declined and fell due to rising aridity over several centuries.[16] Climatically-driven changes to grazing patterns often forced Central Asian tribes to migrate and triggered a domino effect, and more powerful groups displaced weaker ones.[17] The Little Ice Age (1350-1800 AD) weakened populations already reeling from the Bubonic Plague and plunged Europe into wars and famines[18] that could well have killed off 40 per cent of the Central European population.[19] It also stands to reason that regions that are already cold will suffer more from additional cooling, while those that are already warm will suffer more from temperature rises.[20] In a like manner, rising sea levels will affect countries with large, densely populated coastlines. At present, out of the world's 7.6 billion people, four billion live in East, South, and West Asia.[21] Much of this population is concentrated in fertile but warm flood plains or hot (and often humid) coastal areas. While some of the countries in the region like Japan, South Korea, Taiwan, and Singapore are part of the Global North, and others, like the United Arab Emirates (UAE), Qatar, Saudi Arabia, Bahrain, and Kuwait, are rich fossil-fuelled monarchies, nearly 90 per cent of the region is poor or middle-income. Economic growth in countries like India has added to GDP, but inequalities are steep,[22] governance is weak, and corrupt elite capture of decision-making is rife with little hope of corrective impulse arising from the societies in question.

Now imagine a four degrees Celsius increase to average global temperature by 2100, with about half of this warming by 2050. Most of the densely populated areas in India and Pakistan would become uninhabitable for months at a time[23] [24] Water would dry up completely,[25] and the resulting impact on agriculture[26] would be devastating. The top 10 per cent could sit at home with the air-conditioners on, but what would the rest do? And how long could a society facing agricultural collapse be able to pay for its power sector to keep on generating electricity? Not very long, one suspects. Rising sea levels pose another danger. Rich cities, like Boston or London, might well be able to engineer their way out of immediate danger. But South Asian or East Asian cities, reeling from rising temperatures and water shortages, are likely to be sunk, in the literal sense of the term. People will have no choice but to move in search of cooler weather, water and food.

What kind of chaos would be unleashed if, over the next 50 years, half of the world's population finds it impossible to continue living in its existing locations? Will states like China, Brazil, Mexico, India, Pakistan, Iran, Turkey, Egypt, Israel, Vietnam, Thailand, Malaysia, and Indonesia obliterate each other in a desperate quest for living space? Will such states simply collapse under the strain of the climate apocalypse leading to billions of deaths and hundreds of millions of refugees fleeing northwards to Siberia and Europe or southwards to Australia and New Zealand? What will happen to the nuclear arsenals of China, India, Pakistan, North Korea, and Israel amidst all this chaos? Will the Canadians, Russians, Europeans, and Australians open their hearts and diminishing resources to these refugees? Or will they bomb, torpedo, incarcerate, torture, and humiliate refugees and try to secure themselves behind hard borders? As things stand, Australia[27] and the United States[28] already have concentration camps for refugees, while the mood in Europe is shifting in favour of hard borders and not letting people of undesirable origins (i.e., not White) in.[29] These are but a handful of the many unpleasant questions that the crisis of habitability will generate as the intensifying effects of global warming and ecological collapse ravage the world's population.

Real estate, it is popularly said, is all about location. While most of the world stands to horribly lose from environmental disintegration, the warming of the planet will produce, for a few decades at least, new opportunities for exploiting nature in the Arctic, Siberia and Antarctica. The elimination of permafrost at these locations will make these icy wastes habitable, navigable and arable.[30] The geopolitical fulcrum of the world will move to the extreme north and south as the old heartland of human habitation turns into a dead zone. For countries like Russia and Canada, this is a historic opportunity to gain ascendancy. While for Australia, New Zealand, Britain, Scandinavia, and the United States, new spheres of influence and competition are about to emerge, and if this grouping can stay united, it will have definite advantages over Russia.

By shifting population and agricultural production as needed, while deploying military strength and location advantages, these countries could well survive the climate apocalypse. If they do, then the Asian, African, and Latin American dead zones could be left to recover along with any primitive societies that somehow manage to survive in the Global South. This great inversion of the habitable zone would mean that the Global North – having industrialised and modernised by consuming the resources of the Global South[31] – could shield itself to an extent from the effects of the catastrophe that its economic wealth will produce. Certainly, the Americans, Europeans, and Russians have considerable expertise in applying genocidal policies and have profited greatly from them in the past.[32]

There is, however, one major power that has the potential to challenge and upend the Global North's *de facto* final solution to the problem of the Global South. That power is China, situated adjacent to the demographic vacuum of Russia's Siberia. It is in a position to overrun this post-apocalyptic breadbasket by the sheer weight of numbers. Though far poorer than the United States or Canada, China has a ruthless, efficient, and disciplined state imbued with a Darwinian outlook and no illusions about the struggle for survival that lies ahead.[33] At present, China is using its economic strength to secure the world's remaining resources, open communications, and build the infrastructure needed to project power.[34] Building communications into Central Asia and Russia makes sense. Nearly 60 per cent of China's population lives near the coast, and a major redistribution of the population might become necessary as coastal ecology collapses and temperatures and sea levels rise.[35] As climate breakdown intensifies, the Sino-West competition is likely to heat up. Whether this leads to open warfare, a cold war, or some other realignment, China is determined to use all the means at its disposal to ensure national survival.

The shifting of the world's arable zone to the north and the liquidation of most Asian, African, and Latin American populations due to climate apocalypse will lead to a new era of geopolitics for the survivors. Policies aimed at securing national or regional autarchy in the Global North and managing the demise of badly afflicted states in the Global South will define the future even as those societies that manage to endure longer struggle to maintain standards of living and their democratic political dispensations. There are possible countermeasures that states in the developing world can take, but, with the exception of China, none seem to have the vision and internal organisation to manage the emerging crisis.

The first step along what promises to be an incredibly painful path is for the leaders of developing countries to comprehend the totality of the horror that is headed their way. There is, at this stage, no escape from disaster. The planet is dying, and the present-day warm/temperate zones are going to die first. A few more per cent of annual GDP growth between now and 2030 or 2040 will be meaningless in view of the ecological collapse that will have matured in a generation. It is the height of foolishness for developing countries to place any stock in the promises of the rich countries. The fact is that if the developed world had been serious about saving the environment, it would have acted in the 1980s and 1990s. True to form, the wealthy countries are still primarily interested in finding a way to continue business as usual while making token concessions to movements like the Extinction Rebellion.

The second step is to recast all national policies from the perspective of saving the environment and finding ways to offset or manage the effects of climate disasters. This means putting an end to the extraction of local resources for global trade, limiting commercial farming, investing in hardened water resource infrastructure, clamping down on population growth, and moving national economies towards self-sufficiency, dispensing, in the process, with what cannot be locally or regionally produced. All of these steps need to be taken on a total war footing and may necessitate the suspension of such civil and human rights as exist in developing countries. Dictatorships that embrace environmentalism, as Tokugawa Japan did when faced with the collapse of the country's forest cover in the 1700s, might well have a better chance of survival under emerging circumstances.

The third step is to provide maximum logistical and diplomatic support to enlightened opinion in the developed world and help it break through the policy logjam. While it is correct that rich countries with relatively smaller populations and vastly more advanced technical and scientific abilities will be able to manage climate change and possibly survive longer, there is no guarantee of this outcome. Moreover, with greying populations, coping with the economic dislocations caused by climate change will not be easy, even for the wealthiest countries. The greater the success of movements, like the Extinction Rebellion, in rich countries, the better the chances that at least some of the developing world might survive.

The fourth step is to invest in nuclear weapons. These are great equalisers. The experiences of India, Pakistan, Israel, and North Korea testify to the immense strategic value of such weapons. In order to have real strategic bargaining chips, countries like Egypt, Iran, Indonesia, and Turkey need to follow the Indian and Pakistani examples. At the very least, such weapons will deter preemptive strikes by Western powers[36] and build leverage to allow more people from these countries to migrate northwards. There is a chance that if nuclear-armed environmentalist and survivalist regimes emerge in enough of the developing world, the Global North might be compelled to modify its behaviour or at least help save a greater percentage of Asians, Africans, and Latin Americans, from the effects of climate apocalypse.

The world is headed to a new dark age, one that will be unprecedented in its global reach. To survive, let alone thrive, in the geopolitics of a post-apocalyptic world will require clarity and resolve. The challenge is that when a culture is in its high civilisation phase, it is unable to contemplate the dynamics of its downfall rationally. At present, globalisation has produced a high civilisation that is extractive and energy-intensive beyond anything previously experienced. Understanding the links between high civilisation and the downfall that almost invariably follows is critical if humanity is to survive.

The Transience of High-Level Equilibrium and the Inevitability of Downfall

In the second century of the Christian Era, the empire of Rome comprehended the fairest part of the Earth, and the most civilized portion of mankind. The frontiers of that extensive monarchy were guarded by ancient renown and disciplined valor. The gentle but powerful influence of laws and manners had gradually cemented the union of the provinces. Their peaceful inhabitants enjoyed and abused the advantages of wealth and luxury. The image of a free constitution was preserved with decent reverence: the Roman senate appeared to possess the sovereign authority, and devolved on the emperors all the executive powers of government. During a happy period of more than fourscore years, the public administration was conducted by the virtue and abilities of Nerva, Trajan, Hadrian, and the two Antonines. It is the design of this, and of the two succeeding chapters, to describe the prosperous condition of their empire; and afterwards, from the death of Marcus Antoninus, to deduce the most important circumstances of its decline and fall; a revolution which will ever be remembered, and is still felt by the nations of the earth.[1]
- Edward Gibbon (*The Decline and Fall of the Roman Empire*, first published in 1776)

From the earliest historical times to the present day, states and civilisations have risen and fallen. Philosophers, historians, political scientists, and even economists have attempted to explain this phenomenon. While a diverse array of thinkers and perspectives can all agree that rise and fall are ubiquitous features of the human experience, attempts to explain why this pattern exists in the first place have generated a fierce debate that led to the emergence of explanatory models. To Herodotus, the oscillation in human fortune is rooted in the universal human propensity towards hubris, which, once it clouds our ability to make rational decisions, invites nemesis.[2] For Ibn Khaldun, the strengthening or weakening of elite group feeling led to the rise and fall of empires. To Edward Gibbon, diminishing rationality and internal discord drove civilisations to collapse. For more economy-minded thinkers like Paul Kennedy, powers rose when their underlying material and human resources were greater than their political and military commitments, and the decline was the result of these commitments outstripping resources for prolonged periods.[3] These and many other ideas are of immense value to anyone trying to understand the past and present better. In general, analyses of civilisations or empires rising and falling employ the concept of the Golden Age – a period of extraordinary strength, ascendance, harmony, resilience, progress, wealth, and happiness. One can also think of this as a high-level equilibrium that serves as the transitional period between growth and atrophy.

With the benefit of hindsight, it is easy to identify a Golden Age in the histories of fallen empires. An important problem that international relations have attempted to address is the emergence of new powers and whether or not they will overtake established ones.[4] These days China is the subject of much intense speculation in this regard.[5] At the same time, one must consider that for those who lived through the Golden Age, it may not be clear to them that their civilisation or state has peaked. The expectation would rather be to consider the high-level equilibrium as natural and self-perpetuating and therefore normal. Only when calamity strikes that decline in relation to what has gone before allows the distinction to be drawn between periods of greatness and decline.

The onset of a Golden Age may also occur without conscious design or awareness of what is going on. So, when Julius Caesar, struggling for personal survival, reshaped the Roman Republic into a monarchy,[6] neither he nor his detractors believed that they were living through the beginning of Rome's Golden Age. This high-level equilibrium set in as a result of deep structural forces that were pushing and pulling individual actors in different directions. Centuries later, the Arab Empire, in its Umayyad and Abbasid incarnations (AD 660-1258), rose to rule half the known world – from the Indus and Oxus to the Atlantic Ocean.

Today, it seems obvious that these centuries represented the Golden Age of Islam, especially in view of the Mongol cataclysm that engulfed much of the Muslim world between AD 1217 and 1400.[7] Whether this period was actually felt to be a Golden Age of any kind by those living through it – with all its intrigue and massacres – is open to question.

In China, the unification of its core territories under the Legalist Qin dynasty - which persecuted Confucianism in 221 BC, is a historical outcome central to the idea of the country as an ancient civilisation-state. However, the first emperor of the Qin is reviled as an unnecessarily cruel and impious ruler. While the Han dynasty, which seized power in 206 BC, inherited a unified administrative state and kept most of the Qin governance structures in place. It is regarded as China's First Golden Age.[8] In modern times, nostalgia for the age of relative peace before the First World War led to the casting of the late-1800s as Europe's Golden Age. Though given the series of disasters that unfolded between 1914 -1945, one can forgive the Europeans of that period for looking at the generations before as the good old days.

Much as Solon admonished Croesus by trying to explain to him that the happiness of a life can only be fairly judged once it has ended, history teaches us that it is difficult to judge a period of high-level equilibrium while one is still going through it, given the limitations inherent in our perspective. Unfortunately, the totality of the ruin confronting humanity today on account of the operation of a globalised high-level equilibrium is such that we no longer have the luxury of waiting for outcomes before trying to assess what the future holds. Here, history can help us by providing examples of earlier high-level equilibrium civilisations phases and the downfalls in which they ended.

When high-level equilibrium phases are examined, it needs to be understood that we are referring to periods characterised by a relative or absolute intensity in terms of enterprise, material success, and the accumulation of power. Societies that become more powerful than others almost invariably fall into the trap of attributing their good fortune to innate qualities and consequently enjoy moralising. Still, there is little evidence to suggest that greater power is either caused by or otherwise correlated with such conceits. Societies with wildly divergent ethics – from the Aztec Empire built on a theological-political economy of warfare and sacrifice of captives intended to keep the Sun burning,[9] to Muslim empires organised around the institution of the military and administrative slavery,[10] to European Christian empires built on the backs of plantation slaves, the genocide of indigenous peoples, and serfdom[11] established extremely successful polities. It is, therefore, impossible to take claims of moral superiority espoused by the most successful regimes seriously. Some were undeniably worse to their victims, but all were just as surely flawed.

What does need to be taken seriously is the ability of societies entering a high-level equilibrium phase to concentrate power in the hands of their ruling hierarchies. This hierarchical power, whether rooted in religion, bureaucracy, caste, economic wealth, military power, or some combination thereof, as Blair Fix has observed,[12] is the key to understanding the violent and self-aggrandising tendencies of those at the top. Take the pyramids of Egypt as an example. These monuments to the pharaohs demonstrate the ability of the ancient Egyptian state to marshal resources, labour, and organisational ability on a vast scale and then deploy them for long periods of time for the purpose of building very large tombs. Contemporary Egypt's tourism sector relies on the pyramids for much of its pull and would not be the same without these monuments.[13] Herodotus, however, tells us that the systematic coercion needed to build the pyramids left deep psychological wounds on the Egyptian people and that even thousands of years after pyramid building had ceased, the memory of Cheops, the greatest of the builder-pharaohs, was reviled by the common folk.[14] In a like manner, the Great Wall of China[15] was a vast consumer of convict labour,[16] and being sent to the wall could amount to a death sentence for ordinary Chinese. Other empires built fortifications, roads, aqueducts, and irrigation networks and expended resources on military power and conspicuous consumption, leaving in their wake symbolic as well as substantive relics.

When tourists gawk at the pyramids, are inspired by the Taj Mahal, marvel at the precision of Roman infrastructure, or seek to transplant the British industrial revolution to their own countries, it is easy to forget the callousness of the Mughals towards their subjects,[17] the extensive use of slaves by imperial Rome,[18] or the fact that most of the capital used to finance Britain's industrialisation came either from the African slave trade[19] or was looted from dominions of conquest like India.[20] Over 50 years since the NASA moon landing, it remains a remarkable feat of engineering and astrophysics. The objective greatness of this feat cannot be understated. However, one must also keep in mind that over a thousand Nazi German scientists, engineers, and technicians were brought over to the United States and granted amnesty after the Second World War.[21] The person who designed the heavy rocket that took the Apollo landing craft to the moon was Wernher von Braun, a former Nazi *Schutzstaffel* (SS) officer and rocket scientist responsible for designing the Vengeance weapons (V1 and V2), which were the first modern missiles. Von Braun was quite possibly responsible for the deaths of over 20,000 inmates at forced labour camps connected to the Nazi missile program. In other words, all civilisations are extractive, and civilisations in a high-level equilibrium condition are exceptionally extractive. Everything from skilled labour to resources to ideas is drawn into the artifice at the heart of civilisation in such a phase.

Throughout history, civilisations have peaked and, in doing so, drawn upon a greater share of local and regional resources, causing inequality within them to spike and resulting in the concentration of greater power within their ruling hierarchies. For most of history, the horizontal nature of this extractive process placed limits on how large an advanced civilisation could get. Like Rome, Persia, the Arabs, Ottomans, Mughals, and Chinese, empires could get very large and complex through horizontal expansion, but even at their biggest, these empires were, at best, multi-regional powers.

Trade across long distances was possible and did occur fairly regularly, at least for items destined for elite consumption, but economies remained firmly rooted in domestic commerce and agriculture. Under these circumstances, even the most advanced pre-modern empires had to manage practically all of their expenses from the people and territory under their direct physical control. Ensuring this control was itself hugely expensive and required constant vigilance over bureaucracies and local notables employed by imperial centres. The Roman Empire came to be organised around a road network that enabled its 180,000[22] strong standing armies to move across the Mediterranean world with astonishing speed.[23]

Mughal India spent some 80 per cent of its revenues on its military and the rest on maintaining the lifestyle of its service nobility and ruling house.[24] Sometimes the armies and infrastructure backfired, such as when a weak emperor came to power, and the Roman military intervened in politics, or when, during the reign of Marcus Aurelius, a devastating plague killed a fifth of the population, thanks in no small measure, to the excellent road network that allowed the disease to spread widely through the movement of Roman armies being redeployed from the frontier with *Parthia* (now Iran). The great empires of the past existed in a precarious Malthusian and Darwinian balance that often swung against them with devastating results.

This balance eventually collapsed under the weight of internal and external pressures. In the case of the Roman Empire, the concurrent operation of four major upheavals sapped its strength and led to its downfall. First, pressure from tribal peoples on the Roman frontiers intensified after AD 150 due to demographic changes and migrations over which the Romans had no control. Second, the Antonine Plague (referred to above) may have killed some 20 per cent of the population (10-14 million people out of 50-70 million), destabilising the empire from within.[25] Third, after AD 180, a prolonged political crisis set in that saw dozens of emperors raised to the imperial purple only to be killed by the military or rival court factions. And fourth, amidst the onslaught on the borders, the plague, and the endless power struggle in Rome, Christianity spread throughout the empire, promising salvation to the downtrodden.

The hollowing out of Roman military power, population, political order, and ideological appeal combined to generate a dreadful cycle of decline punctuated by briefly successful attempts to stabilise under the occasional strong ruler that still managed to emerge amidst the decline and chaos. In other cases, overpopulation and exhaustion of local resources drove the process of collapse; climate change appears to have played a central role in bringing down the Indus Valley Civilisation, while the waves of Mongol expansion almost annihilated the Muslim and Chinese civilisations.[26] Some who faced the Mongols (like the Ottoman Sultanate) managed to rise again, while others, like the mercurial Tughluq Sultanate of Delhi[27] and the brilliant Song Empire in China (that came tantalisingly close to an industrial revolution), were exterminated.[28]

When a civilisation or empire goes into decline, the consequences for its people are tragic and shattering. In the European context, Ian Morris estimates that Europe did not return to its development level of AD 200 (the end of the *Pax Romana*) till AD 1500 (the beginning of the modern age).[29] Cities like Rome, which had a population of one million in AD 0, had perhaps 40,000-50,000 people by AD 600. In South Asia, the decline and fall of the Mughal Empire led to wars, famines, and dislocations that might have claimed the lives of one-fifth of the region's population. The terrible destruction and suffering unleashed by past collapses may well have appeared to be apocalyptic to those living (and dying) through them.

For all the horror collapse entailed, the story of civilisation managed to continue, revive, and thrive. This was because the destruction was often incomplete and typically operated at the local, regional, or inter-regional level. The decline of one empire or civilisation did not necessarily entail the fall of others. In fact, the decline of the Roman and Persian Empires helped the rise of the Arabs[30] while the decline of Islam's classical civilisation facilitated the rise of the West. This would not be of much comfort to those on the downswing, but it did mean that in a world of basically autarchic regional empires and civilisations dependent upon local resources, downfalls were contained, and revival was, in some cases, a distinct possibility.

The historical pattern of alternating or sequential rise and fall started to change around AD 1500 in ways that were unprecedented. This shift was brought about by five interlocking factors that produced the world's first global civilisation, i.e., the modern West. The first element in this transition was the emergence of classical humanism in the Italian peninsula in the 1300s. The humanist movement reintroduced Christendom to the world of Greco-Roman thought and created a secular space autonomous of the Church wherein scepticism about the world and the human condition could start to take root.[31]

The second ingredient was the rise of seafaring city-states and kingdoms locked in a deadly confrontation with the mighty Ottoman Sultanate. For much of the 1400s and 1500s, the Ottomans enjoyed the upper hand in this conflict. The losses suffered by the Europeans led states like Portugal and Spain to start navigating westwards and southwards in the hope that they might circumvent the Ottomans. These efforts yielded the "discovery" of the Americas, laid the foundations for the Atlantic economy built on the African slave trade, and succeeded in finding alternate routes to Asia. The European age of colonial empire had begun by AD 1509 when Magellan circumnavigated the world.[32]

The third factor was the eruption of the Protestant Reformation (AD 1517). As humanism spread in Northern Europe, it interfaced with Christianity and led to Christian reformism that sought to return the Church to its original message. This was not something the Church hierarchy was interested in, but the stymieing of reform efforts led to a doctrinal schism within western Christianity. This broke the power of traditional religion in much of Europe and helped ensure that humanism and its offshoot, the Scientific Revolution, survived the Roman Catholic Church's furious efforts to stamp out challenges to its authority.[33]

The fourth critical change was the Scientific Revolution which started to take off in the mid-1500s and has not stopped ever since. This revolution upended traditional epistemology and produced an intellectual revolution in Europe that propelled it to first place in terms of science, knowledge, and technology, generating an exponential power deviation in Europe's favour over time.[34]

The fifth major change was that by the mid-1600s, a vast Atlantic economy had emerged, and as European states ruthlessly colonised and exploited the Americas, they gained strategic reserves of resources with which to fund their overseas empires, develop capitalism, and extract the surplus needed to finance a global commercial revolution.[35] It was during this time that the Europeans began their conquest of Asia and Africa as tiny European states like the Netherlands, Portugal, England, and France spread their tentacles all over the world. The rest of the planet was steadily absorbed into a subordinate-periphery type of relationship with the European metropolitan-core countries. As the Europeans imposed favourable terms of trade (soft robbery), openly enslaved and expropriated populations, and perpetrated genocides, they riveted the chains of global civilisation upon everyone else. The continuous operation of this dynamic between 1450 and 1750 produced the critical mass needed to begin Europe's industrial transformation. This was the dawn of the Carbon Age built around using stored energy in the form of fossil fuels to produce controlled combustion, with the residue thrown up into the atmosphere.

It was through European imperialism that a global civilisation emerged. In this civilisation, a relatively small number of winners in the core countries prospered at the expense of everybody else while proclaiming the universality of Western values and approaches. Other cultures and civilisations were placed in a terrible dilemma. They could either read the writing on the wall and embrace modernisation and try to catch up to the West, or they could make piecemeal adjustments trying to preserve their traditions while copying European military techniques, or they could just ignore what was going on. All three alternatives were fraught with danger, though a few countries, like Japan, could make the leap. Other, less fortunate lands fell under the sway of European colonialism, which stimulated organised resistance and the beginnings of nationalism in Asia, Latin America, and Africa.[36] As the European core collapsed in prolonged warfare and economic crisis between 1914 and 1945, the periphery started to gain independence. Many of the elites of the developing world (as it became politely known) were determined to catch up to the West by emulating one of their models of economic growth. This meant increasing GDP and consumption on the Western pattern and ensured that since 1945 more and more of the world would be churned up to either farm, mine, or manufacture, leading to a rapid acceleration of the globalisation process alongside an explosion in the world's population and energy consumption.

The growth of global trade, in particular, encouraged countries to offset local resource shortages and import more stuff, while travel, especially by air and cars for people, and large cargo ships for goods, boomed. Just one person taking a round-trip by air from London to New York produces enough GHGs to melt three square meters of Arctic ice (on average, each American melts 50 square meters of Arctic ice per year).[37] In 2014 there were approximately 100,000 flights per day (nearly 37 million that year), while by 2018, the figure had risen to 45 million flights for the year. Given that 80 per cent of people have never flown[38] (something that airlines want to change), it means that the four to five billion passengers travelling by air every year represent[39] just 20 per cent of the world's population. Mass tourism, one of the greatest achievements of contemporary globalisation, is thus a mass killer of biodiversity and a major driver of global warming.

What makes contemporary globalisation particularly pernicious is that the wealth gap between the richest and poorest nations has grown since 1960.[40] More trade, the opening of financial markets, and rolling back restrictions on the movement of tourists, goods, and services have not altered the balance between the Global North and South in an equitable manner. What it has done is to create a caste of third world globalists whose own fortunes are intimately connected to the power and prosperity of the developed world and fundamentally disconnected from the fortunes of their own people and countries. For these third world globalists, free trade, free movement, and access to the metropolitan centre are the keys to driving their own wealth upwards even as most of their compatriots continue to languish in almost medieval levels of poverty. Post-1990, together with their patrons in the West, "sustainable" growth was pushed by such groups within developing countries, which effectively derailed efforts to protect the environment.[41] With the opening up of China and India in the 1980s and 1990s, the global growth engine received access to new frontiers to explore and exploit and by 2000, human consumption began to push beyond the Earth's carrying capacity. That limit being breached was only a question of when the combination of global warming, biodiversity loss, rising toxicity from waste, and soil degradation would produce a global catastrophe.

The advent of globalisation will, assuming there is anyone left to write history in a century's time, probably be identified as the point of origin for the apocalypse of environmental breakdown that awaits humanity in the next few decades. The early phase of this phenomenon made possible: (the often forced) population exchange, the global networks of trade and created the Atlantic economy. The mature phase saw the emergence of dominant European colonial empires. The modern phase began with the collapse of those empires in the mid-1900s and the advent of developmental paradigms that promised salvation to formerly subjugated peoples. And the contemporary phase, which might well be the last, began with the global triumph of the neoliberal variant of the phenomenon and the intensification of trade, investment, and travel to current unsustainable levels. The globalisation-induced collapse of the Earth's habitability is a catastrophe so comprehensive in its scope that civilisation's story is likely coming to an end. In the past, local, regional, and inter-regional collapses were devastating but remained compartmentalised due to distances and geography. The exhaustion of local resources also typically occurred over many generations, while more sudden upheavals, like invasions and plagues, could lead to migrations into other habitable zones. But global civilisation is extremely vulnerable to disruption due to its interdependence, complexity and intensity. And if the Earth becomes uninhabitable, then there is nowhere else to go. Of course, the great powers will fight it out for pieces of the Arctic or the Antarctic, but even if they manage to move some of their people into the dwindling areas that are habitable, their present national existences will be over. The people in the lower decks of "SS Globalisation" (the Global South) will drown first, and those in the upper decks (the Global North) may last a little longer, but if the whole ship sinks, then everyone meets the same end. A few million or even tens of millions of humans might still survive amidst the ruins of their planet in increasingly dystopian or primitive and isolated conditions. But then again, civilisation, as we understand it, will be over, everywhere, more or less simultaneously. This brings us to an interesting problem – that of Dark Age governance during and after climate breakdown.

VII

Orders of Darkness: Government & Post-Government Amidst the Ruins

Last night I passed by the ruins of Tus;
And saw that an owl had taken the place of the peacock.
I asked, 'What news from these ruins?
It answered, 'The news is – alas, alas!'[1]
– Shahid Balkhi (Persian poet and thinker, d. AD 935)

They say the Lion and the Lizard keep The Courts where
Jamshyd gloried and drank deep: And Bahram, that great
Hunter – the Wild Ass
Stomps over his Head, but cannot break his Sleep.[2]
– Omar Khayyam (Persian polymath, b. 1048, d. 1131)

From *Mad Max* and *Blade Runner* to numerous zombie horror franchises, fictional portraits of the kinds of outcomes that can emerge after collapse have terrified and entertained audiences for decades. While the futures projected by fiction are often horrifying, they are not nearly as awful as the history of actual collapses and their aftermaths. What makes historical collapses so dreadful is that they were real and that millions, or hundreds of millions of people, endured their effects, with many failing to survive the experience.

The dark ages of the past could last centuries, and recovery, if at all possible, was halting and uncertain. These tragedies of the past provide valuable clues as to how societies and states are likely to respond to the comprehensive downfall soon to be realised on account of the breakdown of the Earth's habitability. The kind of orders that will emerge in a world of climate catastrophe, resource depletion, and biodiversity loss are likely to be far harsher and stranger than the darkest dystopias of the past.

Arguably the most successful post-apocalyptic dystopia to have existed was the medieval theocracy of the Roman Catholic Church (AD 600-1500). It lasted nearly a thousand years, retarded the recovery of European culture and civilisation, and ultimately collapsed in large parts of Europe in the wake of the Protestant Reformation. In its glory days, the Roman Church held about one-third of Europe's farmland as fiefs, employed its police and armed forces, maintained a monopoly on learning, and operated the West's only centralised continent-spanning bureaucratic hierarchy. This hierarchy was so powerful that for a thousand years, kings, nobles, and commoners lived in awe of the ecclesiastical power[3] whose authority trumped all others in the gangster's paradise that was the Medieval West.

The Church emerged as Europe's most powerful agency in the wake of the Roman Empire's descent into chaos. For some part of that decline, Christians were viewed as enemies of the state (which they were in the epistemological, if not the political sense) and subject to sporadic persecution. From the classical Roman perspective, the problem was that the decline of the empire's secular fortune was being propelled by demographic trends, military over-extension, and political chaos, all of which enhanced the appeal of Christianity.[4] With Europe experiencing massive population decline, de-urbanisation, and barbarian invasions, the Church, by converting both locals and invaders to its doctrines, was able to extend Christendom as the old Roman world fell apart.

Medieval Christendom had five characteristics that are relevant to understanding the kind of responses future collapse might entail. First, the Church promoted and benefited from a mindset that saw the secular world as inherently unworthy of human endeavour. Instead, the pious ideal was a life of seclusion from worldly affairs that would allow good Christians to dedicate their time to the pursuit of personal salvation. In this manner, moral and psychological escapism became central to the ethos of Christian Europe. Second, the Church obliterated or marginalised any source of intellectual authority or knowledge that did not have its approval. This included the physical destruction of Greco-Roman places or learning, persecution of non-conformists, and propaganda.[5] This epistemological totalitarianism allowed the Church to control what people thought and render them unwilling or unable to contemplate any approach towards "reality" not based on religious doctrines.

Third, the Church was willing to legitimise barbarian warlords and Roman aristocrats in exchange for their acceptance of its intellectual and moral authority. This enabled the Church to establish a field presence that was used to shape the religious worldview of the masses without, however, providing them with direct access to the sources of Christian doctrine. Fourth, the Church, based on the first three points, was able to extract taxes, lands, military service, donations, etc., for itself while absolving itself of any real responsibility for the material wellbeing of its human flock. And fifth, the Church integrated itself into the feudal caste system as the first estate. Members of the theocratic caste enjoyed immunity to local courts and operated as autonomous agents of the Papacy. The administrative enervation, intellectual regression, and political fragmentation of post-Roman Europe eminently suited the Church.

The combination of these five elements enabled the Church to preside over the ruins of the post-Roman world for nearly a millennium. In that post-apocalyptic set-up, feudal lords endlessly fought each other; wars, plagues, and famines ravaged Europe. Attempts to question the Church led to ferocious persecution. The inquisitor, the censor, and the crusader were the razor's edge of this benighted order. One example of this, which provides one of the first historical accounts of planned and systematic genocide, is the Albigensian Crusade of the 1200s. The Albigensians were a Christian sub-sect that rejected the material extravagance of the Church hierarchy. After bureaucratic methods failed to secure their obedience, the Papacy declared them heretics and launched a Crusade against them. Crusaders were absolved of any sins committed in furtherance of the divine commands of the Church and could help themselves to the property of the slaughtered. Some 200,000 Albigensians were killed,[6] while their leadership was burned alive. This drove the sect underground, where it eventually petered out.

Interestingly, the Church got the French king to foot the bill for the military aspect of this persecution. This was not an isolated incident but a recurrent pattern in medieval Christendom arising from the single-minded determination of the Church leadership to preserve its hegemony in Europe's Dark Ages dystopia.[7] The Spanish Inquisition, the Counter-Reformation, the alliance with slavers and the legitimisation of genocidal policies in the Americas (barring the occasional pangs of conscience) helped make the Church Europe's most formidable actor until the French Revolution.[8] At the same time, medieval Christendom did possess an underlying logic. Born into a world of secular failure and contraction, the Church sold the promise of a better afterlife for all who accepted its authority in exchange for a large share of Europe's dwindling resources, which enabled the ecclesiastical hierarchy to live better than others in this world. To the traumatised, miserable, and oppressed, the Church offered hope – not in this life, but the next – and a means of rationalising suffering.

The implications of this historical example for the future are profound. As humanity moves towards a world of environmental collapse, states and societies are going to experience secular failure on a scale far greater than the fall of the Roman Empire. As people are progressively traumatised by the deaths of loved ones, the loss of their homes, the infertility of their farmlands, the increasing heat, water shortages, hunger, and the return of the uncontrolled disease, they will struggle to cope with and make sense of their suffering. The totality of the secular collapse, likely to arise from the Earth becoming largely uninhabitable for humans, will eliminate any scope for secular means of redemption for the vast majority of the people. Amidst such conditions of extreme stress, the revival of traditional religions or the emergence of new death cults like Islamic State of Iraq and Syria (ISIS) are inevitable.[9] Societies that are already religious might lapse into theocracy and fundamentalism. More secular societies are vulnerable to ideologies like fascism and might relapse into overt racism. Such worldviews would thrive in a period of economic contraction, social decay, and intensifying conflict.

While the return of theocracy is one outcome that is likely in societies experiencing collapse, another possibility is the return of totalitarianism rooted in non-religious ideologies. In the West and the materially developed societies of East Asia, an updated version of fascism could be the way of the future. This assessment is not without precedent in world history. Fascism, after all, did emerge as a major political force in the years after the First World War and the disillusionment, poverty, chaos, and brutalisation unleashed by that conflict created festering conditions for radicalism to thrive. Left-wing totalitarianism found expression in the birth of the Soviet Union, while the right-wing variety emerged in the form of Mussolini's Italy, Hitler's Germany, and Hirohito's Japan. Even countries that remained democratic, like Britain and the United States, saw a surge in racist right-wing politics. In the United States, the Jim Crow South was, in fact, a white supremacist and practically authoritarian entity within the larger body politic. As is generally the case, the rise of fascism in Germany, Italy, and Japan was driven by powerful stirrings of nationalism, disappointment with the previous generation of leaders, and a desire to assert state power on the international stage. Ultra-right-wing nationalists tapped into these sentiments to propel their countries towards a Social Darwinist and predatory outlook that enabled crimes against their own and other peoples.[10]

The basic mechanics of the fascist outlook revolved around insensitivity to the suffering they inflicted on others. The first ingredient required to nurture this outlook was a sense of racial, ethnic, or ideological superiority that made others less human. The easiest source of this kind of thinking for fascists in the 1900s was racial nationalism, though religion could also serve a similar purpose. The second ingredient was the belief that the world had conspired to deny them their rightful place in the sun. The third component was to define that rightful place in terms of internal purity and external power, linking the two in a causal relationship. This would have the effect of excluding large groups within the domestic population, deeming them inferior and disloyal and thereby justifying persecution and confiscation of their wealth. The fourth building block saw the world as too small for accommodation or peaceful exchange and coexistence. Instead, only the fascist powers could be allowed to win, and their destiny was to enjoy a monopoly on the fruits of success. The success of any other polity was an affront to fascist greatness. The resulting militarism, permanent war hysteria, and intense jealousy of others strengthened the xenophobic tendencies that fascism fed off of. And last, though by no means least, was the idea that the only way to save society from decay and collapse was to reassert masculinity, reclaim unapologetically traditional patriarchal norms that treated women as chattel, and subordinate the family to the state by making its primary objective the production of more (male) fascists.

At present, neo-fascist and crypto-fascist movements are sweeping the world. Trump, Modi, Xi, Putin, al-Sisi, MBS, Erdogan, Bolsonaro, Le Pen, Orban, Brexit, the Thai military junta, Bangladesh's Awami League, and Burma are just some of the more prominent instances of the return of xenophobic right-wing identity politics. Each in its own way represents the reassertion of national chauvinism, the rejection of common humanity, and a growing insensitivity to the plight of the environment. That such movements are thriving is no surprise. Growing socioeconomic inequality within societies, wrought by neoliberal globalisation, facilitates identity politics as elites use their control of the media to divert public anger and frustration towards religious, ethnic, or racial sentiments. Such movements promise to restore national greatness and purity and help corporate plunder and elite capture by making cooperation within and between societies harder to sustain. In doing so, they help ensure that the kind of global response needed to combat global warming and ecological decay will not be able to materialise. And since any effective response to the environmental crisis will necessitate a crackdown on corporate plunder and plutocratic capture of decision-making, it suits the top one per cent that profit from the status quo.

This being said, today's right-wing authoritarians are still operating on a habitable planet. The deterioration in the Earth's habitability is expected to start asserting itself on a scale sufficient to disrupt human societies by the end of the 2020s and intensify every subsequent year until most of the present habitable zone is rendered dead by the 2070s. As this process unfolds, resource constraints become severe, and economic contraction sets in, authoritarian tendencies are likely to become totalitarian, as harsher and harsher measures are needed to keep elite extraction going. The ability of a new wave of fascist regimes to compete in the kind of chaos that is going to result from environmental breakdown will depend in part on new technology. In the early 20th century, suppressing and brainwashing populations took a lot of physical effort. Tracking what people were doing, saying, and thinking required layers of informers, bureaucracies, and lots of resources. It was also highly imperfect, given that targets of surveillance could modify their behaviour, and those engaged in snooping around could let selfish motives influence what they reported. Moreover, the mere fact that the state enjoyed a monopoly of information made people wary of official narratives – as evidenced by the refreshingly irrepressible brand of Russian jokes about Soviet communism. Powerful states like the Soviet Union or Maoist China could compel conformity through violence and terror and more subtle forms of administrative control, but only at a high price in terms of economic cost, public morale, and expanding the heavy foot of the government.

Today, things are very different, thanks to the Internet, AI, big data mining, and the mobile phone revolution. Anyone who is on the Internet, or has a mobile phone, can be hacked and tracked at all times. Our behaviour generates mass quantities of data. In the "free" world, citizens surrender this data voluntarily to big corporations[11] in exchange for services. In the un-free world, such as China, all data is state property, and there is no operational concept of privacy. In most other countries, intelligence services have the resources to locate and hack any person of interest even if they cannot manage the Chinese level of control.

As computing power inexorably increases, keeping tabs on people will become easier, sometimes with comical results, such as when a young computer enthusiast revealed the location of American military bases by accessing the data from a popular fitness app.[12] The false news epidemic, in the meanwhile, is debilitating and polarising public discourse even in the most advanced countries. Since there is no centralised source of false news, unlike in the old days of state monopolies on broadcast and print, millions of people are duped each day into sharing such stories. Even the most vigilant social media user is susceptible to spreading false news if what they see conforms to their existing opinions.[13]

Organised actors like political parties, corporations, advertisers, and governments have learned to take advantage of this. Troll armies can inflict tremendous psychological pain on dissidents without any need for physical intimidation. Rapidly re-sharing posts, regardless of their authenticity, can cause the message to go viral. Using the data mined from people can help campaigns and states shape public opinion. Minimal selective targeting of people in real life can have a dramatically greater effect because if the target shares their experience, it will inhibit countless others, and if they start censoring themselves, then the desired outcome from the oppressor's perspective has been achieved. Any kind of outrageous, ignorant, or anti-social behaviour or advocacy can spread far and wide before it is shut down, while bots and people running dummy accounts can do a lot of the leg work of disinformation campaigns.[14]

The Rolls Royce of Dark Age information dystopia is the ingenious social credit system pioneered by China. Through this system, the government can rate its citizens for loyalty and reliability and mete out rewards and punishments in terms of access to services.[15] This system would be very helpful in allocating dwindling resources to loyal citizens in a future of environmental collapse. Far from empowering people, Information Technology (IT) and AI have placed the ultimate weapons in the hands of governments and corporations that can be employed to influence what people think and maintain social control.[16] The day may not be far off when babies are implanted with microchips that communicate vital information to remote servers. What makes this process so hard to resist is the sheer convenience of being connected. Everything from being able to pay your bills from home, network with thousands of people, enjoy free telephone calls, and order groceries can be managed from home.[17]

Amidst conditions of global heating, it may well become inadvisable for people in large parts of the world to step outside for months at a time, making these IT tools essential to human survival. Imagine a world where the government operated robots/drones roam otherwise deserted streets delivering rations to people confined to their homes due to the extreme heat and toxicity of the outdoors and/or unforeseen deadly diseases. Such people would be completely at the mercy of their state. Totalitarianism in the past was a clumsy and heavy-handed exercise, but automated social credit systems, combined with complete monitoring of human behaviour, would allow for the total dismantlement of the private sphere. A fascist dystopia of the mid-2000s would be able to exercise greater control with a lighter footprint while providing convenience and protection against the effects of environmental deterioration to its loyal citizens. Allowing various iterations of Amazon's Alexa to take over our lives is not just about shopping from the convenience of one's couch. It is about giving corporations and governments the ability to read our minds while cutting us off from other people. This is a power that the police state apparatus of the KGB and Gestapo would have envied.

What are governments and corporations doing with the enormous unregulated power of being able to read our minds? For the former, the desired result is control of the narrative, while for the latter, it is making more money, diminishing the human component of their organisation, and inhibiting collective response to the ecological ruin neoliberal capitalism is bringing about.[18] It does not take much to imagine a fascistic world in which states ration resources and services based on loyalty while corporations continue to reap profits by catering to the top 10 per cent while everyone else struggles to survive amidst climate apartheid. In many ways, this craven new world of bot and troll powered narratives, and convenience-driven elite consumption is already here. The intensification of the Earth's crisis of habitability in the coming decades will destroy the veneer of civility and humane pretensions which most states and companies still publicly espouse.

An essential component of navigating a world of ecological instability will be controlling the majority of the population – the ones who will suffer horrendously – so as not to disturb the rich and the powerful. Internal systems of concentration camps, the incitement of mass violence against minorities and dissidents, warfare against weaker states, genetic tampering, reverting to pre-industrial patriarchy, the return of slavery, the institutionalisation of discrimination based on race, caste, and creed, and the end of human rights as a practice and a legitimate concept, are just some of the instruments of control that will have to be employed. A variation on the theme of a statist fascist dystopia is a corporate dystopia in which, as the world's habitability tanks, plutocrats seize control of territory and resources and develop their own armies and police forces to maintain control.[19] In conditions of extreme scarcity, even if billions perish, such corporate enterprises could still make money while destroying the world's remaining resources. Given the historic closeness between big business and fascism and the corporations' need for a government to maintain a semblance of order, the more likely scenario is that the fascist state and corporate interests work together.[20]

While many states are well on the way to becoming IT-powered fascist dystopias, others could evolve into relatively more benign and rational environmentalist dictatorships. Smaller and highly advanced states like New Zealand or the Scandinavian countries are already in the process of subordinating national policymaking to scientific advice. As the ecological crisis worsens and piecemeal adaptations fail to cut it, more and more authority might end up being transferred to scientific advisory bodies that would dictate measures to contain the damage. This kind of scientific technocracy would effectively subordinate the authority of parliaments and cabinets to its advice.

Like fascist regimes, environmentalist authoritarians motivated by the sense that they must do whatever it takes to save the planet will impose restrictions on what people can do. Assigning everyone a carbon budget, heavy carbon taxes, limiting trade and travel, a massive public works program aimed at transitioning to carbon-neutrality on a war footing, universal basic income, massive public borrowing and confiscatory taxation on the wealthy are some measures that will be deemed necessary. Environmental crimes would merit harsher punishments, while global trade and investment would collapse as economies reorient themselves towards local production and consumption. The management of this transition will necessitate a much stronger, more authoritarian, and intrusive state with a lot more bureaucracy. Paying for this in conditions of de-globalisation of trade, shrinking economies, and flight of capital will not be easy and could accelerate economic collapse and lead to worse shortages and more extreme rationing. There is every chance that the only way to deal with rightwing opposition will be to declare emergencies, suspend civil rights, and allow mobs of enraged environmentalists to mete out "climate justice" to "climate criminals".

This could also escalate into inter-generational warfare as those presently under the age of 40, justifiably enraged by the selfishness and heedlessness of baby boomers, start to liquidate older people. Since the rightwing in countries like Britain and the United States is better armed than the centre and left, countries with complex and divided demographics could well break up into liberal and conservative states. Scotland could secede from the United Kingdom, while liberal coastal states might find it impossible to stay within the Unites States dominated by a racist anti-environmentalist white minority entrenched in power through gerrymandering and control of the Supreme Court.

Thus far, the options discussed have presumed that a semblance of state order will survive in a future dominated by environmental collapse. This might hold true in the West, East Asia, and a few other states. However, climate catastrophe will lead to state failure for much of the planet. Already weaker, poorer, less legitimate, and less organised states in the developing world are facing dire consequences on account of ecocide.

Failing to respond effectively to the contemporary effects of global warming, local resource depletion, and runaway population growth, many states in South Asia, West Asia, Africa, and Latin America will not live to see 2100.

As state capacity plummets in relative and then absolute terms, such societies are likely to revert to caste, kinship, and tribal affiliations to survive. Those people who do not have strong primordial networks will perish during the initial stages of collapse. Those who have access to such networks will be forced back into a strictly hierarchical relationship with their kinship group or tribal leaders. Whatever little gain the developing world has experienced regarding women's rights and children's rights will evaporate as temperatures rise and states and economies fall. Slavery, child marriage, and the open treatment of women and children as property of tribal males will return without the pretence of public order to restrain such violations.

Given how much worse climate change will affect women, it is mortifying to see coal mining operations in Pakistan being praised for employing female truck drivers. In these conditions, it will not be possible to immunise children, send them to school, or provide basic healthcare. The gains in control of communicable diseases, sanitation, and population welfare made possible by state intervention will be reversed within a generation. Life expectancy will revert to medieval levels as disease, starvation, and violence destroy populations. Some states which have significant military power, such as India and Pakistan, or smaller, more developed populations such as Bhutan and Sri Lanka, might manage to preserve some kind of state order in their metropolitan areas for a few more decades. By 2100, as temperatures soar by four degrees, water resources disappear, and the population collapses, it is not likely that any "state" worth the name will be left standing in the Global South.

The implications for governance arising from ecocide are stark. It is highly unlikely that any kind of liberal political order and economic system as these terms are understood today will survive more than two generations into the future. Right-wing fascist, theocratic regimes, left-wing green dictatorships, or reversion to tribalism are the types of political and social orders likely to survive during the coming ecological crunch. Isolated communities of survivalists could endure for long periods of time in highly favourable locations though it is not clear that they would do so for long enough to allow the Earth to return to some sort of pre-industrial stability. Even more radical outcomes such as genetically engineered humans or sentient AI taking control cannot be ruled out. The latter, in particular, would be largely immune to the effects of global warming. This new Dark Age would last at least 1,000 years, which is how long it would take the Earth to naturally revert to pre-industrial revolution levels of atmospheric carbon if all emissions ceased today. Of course, emissions are not going to cease anytime soon, and with the polar ice caps melting 70 years ahead of what was predicted, the release of even more GHGs could lead to a situation where it would take tens of thousands of years for concentrations to return to pre-industrial levels.

Conclusion: Is There a Way Out?

All life on Earth, including humans, stands at the brink of downfall on account of deficiencies in human nature that have been magnified by the oscillations of historical experiences. Human intelligence does not so much appear to be an evolutionary advantage but an aberration responsible for the presently unfolding mass extinction. The human appetite for convenience, longevity and more material stuff has mined the environment to exhaustion. The human propensity towards optimism ensured that decades of warnings from scientists and philosophers that the world was hurtling towards ecological disintegration were dismissed. In order to manage the effects of industrialisation and globalisation, humanity sorely needed the wisdom and sense of proportion of Solon. Regrettably, an assortment of hubristic Croesus-like leaders aided and abetted by growth cultists operating in the tradition of Pangloss held sway and continue to rule nearly everywhere. History teaches us that the inaneness of the *Homo Sapiens* is such that the capacity for insight is a very limited one and that the chances of getting those with the requisite understanding into positions of authority are slim to none.

A predictable question that arises after the doom and gloom of the preceding pages is to ask if there is any way out of humanity's self-inflicted predicament. The incorrigible optimists like Pangloss would have people believe that this is still the best of all possible worlds and that science and technology have an ace up their sleeves that will dispel the adverse effects of human activity on the environment. Other, more conservative types might still genuinely believe, in the face of all evidence, that all these fluctuations are natural and will sort themselves. Sadly, for both optimists and conservatives, the tipping points already crossed due to human activities are so disastrous that no technical solution can by itself rescue life on Earth.

Each fantastic solution, like carbon capture, or a Green New Deal, will consume resources and energy that the Earth can no longer tolerate. And even if the funding and resources were not an issue, the technology was perfect, and all that was needed was to give the order, the 9 to 12 year timeframe left to make the changes is insufficient to move entire societies towards genuine ecological regeneration. What is needed to change the way states and societies think about environmental issues and make them realise that only hard choices lie ahead and that this will entail many sacrifices.

To survive beyond 2100, we need to abandon all hope and all pretence that things can continue as they have thus far. A new approach is needed – one fundamentally at odds with what passes for normalcy today. And this shift needs to be brought about in 3,000 days, or the darkest scenarios articulated by scientists will certainly come to pass. So here are seven lessons for our final century that, if learned and applied, might just allow life on Earth and, incidentally, human civilisation to continue for millennia to come.

The first lesson is that it is time to start seeing ourselves not as individuals operating in a present-minded vacuum but as tiny pieces of a continuum of a great story that stretches far back into time. In other words, to survive, humans must learn to think in historical time, see themselves in historical terms, and act as if the future of civilisation deserves to last at least as long as its history. The temporal frame of reference for policies and actions needs to be centuries, not days, months, and years. The mental discipline it takes to think in such structural terms is immense. With the exception of China, no major power has a tradition of secular thought that engages with reality in historical terms, and even in the Chinese example, the application of this approach has been sketchy at best. In the past, cultures had the option of muddling through if for no other reason than their impact on the environment was not as catastrophic as it is today. Modern civilisation desperately needs to acquire a heightened historical consciousness. There are modern thinkers like Fernand Braudel, Jared Diamond, Peter Turchin, Roman Krznaric, and Ian Morris whose perspectives manifest the approach that political leaders and mainstream pundits need to adopt.

If we start to really think historically about our problems, then the second lesson, the need to abandon our absurd fascination with economic growth, becomes self-evident. Growing an economy by converting natural assets into material ones at a rate faster than the former can regenerate is ultimately suicidal. Our mainstream economists remain confident that pollution, biodiversity loss, and global warming, while bad news, is not as important as more GDP. The world has also been sold on the desirability of global trade and travel. And even though the dominant growth framework followed for the past 40 years has disproportionately benefited the top one per cent, the prescription for all ills remains yet more growth.

If human civilisation is going to survive, there is no choice but to move towards a stationary state or some version of managed de-growth. Instead of growth, the objective of economic planning will have to change to well-being and from "sustainable growth" (which is a fantasy) to the regeneration of nature. This shift might actually be easier for countries in the Global South that have been badly let down by the dominant economic model. Countries like India, Pakistan, Bangladesh, Sri Lanka, and Burma could actually follow the example of small states like Bhutan and New Zealand by shifting the emphasis to well-being and helping nature recover. These and most other states in the Global South have literally nothing to lose by stepping off the collective suicide train that is contemporary capitalism.

If any country decides to abandon economic growth as an objective, the challenge it will face will be to manage a holistic transition to an ecologically regenerative and well-being oriented system. Here, the historical tendency to make bad decisions in the face of opposition by vested interests may well derail the noblest policy initiatives. In both democratic and autocratic states, as well as hybrid models like Pakistan, pushing through the reforms needed requires sustained leadership commitment, a critical mass of popular support, and solid administration. The pressure needed to push for change will have to endure for at least 20 years, and, on top of it, enough large countries will have to sign on for it to have a much-needed global impact. Brazil, for instance, can derail efforts at containing global warming through reforestation and restoration of meadows by allowing more of the Amazon to be cleared for farming and mining - something that its present fascistic government is intent on doing.

The experience of wartime mobilisation in the first half of the 20th century indicates that both democracies and autocracies are capable of the required level of mass mobilisation to combat threats like climate change. The difficulty lies in convincing governments to go to that level of mobilisation in order to save the planet rather than for killing each other. Here, major developing countries like China, India, Indonesia, Pakistan, Nigeria, South Africa, Egypt, Turkey, Burma, Thailand, Mexico and Brazil could get things started by declaring environmental emergencies and start implementing policies aimed at securing nature within their national boundaries.

Admittedly, the administrative effectiveness of regenerative policies will be a concern, but, as Pakistan's reforestation effort shows, even a poor country with a tottering bureaucracy can, if the political will is there, tackle major environmental problems head-on. The lesson to be learned here is that all other issues that states currently think are problems are nothing compared to the effects of ecocide. For India and Pakistan to keep squabbling over Kashmir, trade, terrorism, and who has the best mangoes, they need to be physically around. Neither is likely to survive the crisis of habitability wrought by climate change and local environmental depletion.

If enough states understand that dominant models of economic growth are senseless and that moving towards regenerative and well-being-centred policies is the key to survival, they will be ready to learn the fourth lesson. This is to take a page out of Churchill's book and tell their people how bad things are and how much worse they will get before they might start to get better. Technological optimism and wishful thinking need to be banished from policy discourse and public pronouncements on the ecological crisis. People need to be told the truth by their governments. The Earth is dying, human activity is killing it, and powerful corporate vested interests that want to make more money before everything collapses have delayed effective action until it is almost too late.

What lies ahead is a struggle for survival like no other in history. And like Churchill, the world's leaders need to tell their people that for the next 20 years, they will have nothing to offer but sacrifice and that without a victory in this struggle, there will be no survival. They must also tell their people that there is a good chance that these efforts will fail but that the only real hope lies in making the sacrifices necessary to break with business as usual because an environmentally ruined world will not only be unlivable for billions, it will not be worth living in for those who survive. As Zhou Enlai explained to his colleagues at the beginning of China's communist revolution (July 1927): "If we do not fight, we surely die. If we fight, we may die, but we may win."[1] To save human civilisation, what is needed is not false hope but heroic realism in the pattern of Churchill, Zhou Enlai, or Leonidas.

The fifth lesson that the world needs to learn is that as resource crunches and climate change hits, as they must, even in the most optimistic scenarios, scarcity will spike, and the intuitive response of each major power or bloc will be to pull inwards and consolidate control over its own sphere of influence. Growing insularity and xenophobia are very human responses to danger and shortages. But if states give in to these impulses, they will plunge the world into apocalyptic geopolitics. Any major military conflict or a new cold war at this critical juncture will dramatically add to GHG emissions and ecological destruction and divert energies away from regenerative policies.

While cutting back on global trade and travel and moving towards localisation of manufacturing and services will end economic globalisation, greater political, scientific, environmental, humanitarian, and administrative cooperation across national and regional boundaries will be needed. Falling into a new cold war, stumbling into a hot war, or otherwise reducing international cooperation will hasten the process of downfall. There is a tremendous responsibility on the shoulders of the current generation of political and military leaders to understand that the real enemy is ecocide, not each other, and only intense global cooperation will be able to pull humanity out of a tailspin.

The sixth lesson is that civilisation is passing through the end of the high-level equilibrium phase of globalisation and capitalism. History teaches that such phases do not last forever, however much the elites benefiting from them would like them to, and that there is a natural tendency towards decline and fall. In the past, civilisations lacked awareness that they were going through such periods or thought that high-level equilibrium was normal and went into shock when the decline began.

This time, however, civilisation can manage the decline of its present high-level equilibrium in an orderly fashion and deliberately transition towards regenerative frameworks. The top one per cent will look back upon the period from 1975-2025 as the golden age of capital, from which they derived disproportionate and inequitable benefit at the cost of future generations and billions of working people all over the world. But now it is time to start paying the bill for the party that neoliberal baby boomers and their apologists threw themselves. Perhaps, over the next several hundred years, the pursuit of regenerative policies will enable the Earth to recover, more equitable prosperity to descend on a much smaller human population while continuing to expand scientific knowledge at an exponential rate, and a far better and more enduring high-level equilibrium in the form of an advance eco-utopia might emerge. The next 80 years will require the dismantling of neoliberal globalisation and, if necessary, forcible de-carbonisation of society and economy to realise this possibility and create a future truly worth having.

The final lesson, at least for the purpose of this collection of essays, is that in the years and decades to come, political orders and governance structures will be severely tested. Many states will fail due to environmental collapse, while others might evolve into dark dystopian versions of themselves. Dystopias that deny the humanity of others and seek to employ racial or religious identities as weapons while promising "solutions" based on repression and hatred are a real possibility. These cannot be ruled out even in advanced liberal democracies. But there is an alternative that might actually work. It is the Platonic concept, from *The Republic*, of the rule of the qualified, as opposed to rule by the popular, rich or powerful. In view of the crisis of habitability facing the Earth, the most qualified people to make decisions are scientists, philosophers, and technical experts. The trouble is that people with expertise are generally not listened to on broader policy questions. That might be fine under normal conditions, but the severity of the ecological crisis is such that all governments need to constitute advisory bodies of experts to meet the environmental challenge and treat the advice given as binding.

Taken together, and they ought to be considered a package deal, these seven lessons, if learned and acted upon, might well help humanity and life on Earth survive long past 2100. There is still time to mend our wicked ways and make better and wiser decisions and meet the challenge of the environmental crisis. It is also important to bear in mind that if humans cannot learn from history even now, then by 2100, there probably will not be anyone left to repeat it.

NOTES

Introduction: The Anatomy of Downfall

[1] "Our analysis found that a significant proportion of the world's population—over 40 per cent, primarily located in Africa and South Asia—simply do not have 3.75 dollars to spend on food every day. This amount is far above the international poverty line of 1.90 dollars." Anna Herforth, "Three Billion People cannot afford Healthy Diets. What does this mean for the next Green Revolution?," *Center for Strategic and International Studies*, Commentary, September 23, 2020, https://www.csis.org/analysis/three-billion-people-cannot-afford-healthy-diets-what-does-mean-next-green-revolution (Accessed: May 7, 2022).

[2] "The findings in the report indicate that as of 2011, 2.6 trillion dollars of developing countries' private wealth is held in tax havens, over half of the 4.4 trillion dollars of total developing country assets in these same jurisdictions. Sub-Saharan Africa's assets held in tax havens grew at an annualized rate of over 20 per cent from 2005 to 2011, a faster rate than that of any other region either developed or developing." See the Global Financial Integrity findings at http://gfintegrity.org/press-release/new-report-on-unrecorded-capital-flight-finds-developing-countries-are-net-creditors-to-the-rest-of-the-world/ (Accessed: May 6, 2022).

[3] Developed countries are responsible for 79 per cent of cumulative Greenhouse Gas Emissions since 1850. See the Center for Global Development's findings at https://www.cgdev.org/media/who-caused-climate-change-historically (Accessed: May 6, 2022).

[4] As per the United Nations, the world faces Climate Aparthied in the short-term and medium-term, threatening to wipe out improvements to living standards achieved by developing countries since 1945. See https://news.un.org/en/story/2019/06/1041261 (Accessed: May 6, 2022).

[5] Pew conducted a survey (2020-2021) that revealed a generational divide in terms of environmental awareness, with younger generations more concerned about climate change: "when asked about engaging with climate change content online, those in Gen Z are particularly likely to express anxiety about the future. Among social media users, nearly seven-in-ten Gen Zers (69%) say they felt anxious about the future the most recent time they saw content about addressing climate change. A smaller majority (59%) of Millennial social media users report feeling this way the last time they saw climate change content; fewer than half of Gen X (46%) and Baby Boomer and older (41%) social media users say the same." See: https://www.pewresearch.org/science/2021/05/26/gen-z-millennials-stand-out-for-climate-change-activism-social-media-engagement-with-issue/ (Accessed: May 6, 2022).

[6] For an analysis of the Whiteness (and classism) of climate change activism, see Sarah Jacquette Ray, "Climate Anxiety is an Overwhelmingly White Phenomenon," in the *Scientific American*, online, March 21, 2021, https://www.scientificamerican.com/article/the-unbearable-whiteness-of-climate-anxiety/ (Accessed: May 6, 2022).

[7] For details on the UK government's strategy with reference to Net Zero by 2050, see its official policy paper: "Net Zero Strategy: Build Back Greener," released in 2021, https://assets.publishing.service.gov.uk/government/uploads/system/uploads/attachment_data/file/1033990/net-zero-strategy-beis.pdf (Accessed: May 6, 2022).

[8] In 2012, scientists estimated that Arctic ice could disappear by 2090. But in 2020, the speed of the ice melt and temperature rise in the Arctic led scientists to revise their projections to 2035. As the world heats up, the climate system is reacting unpredictably. Alejandra Borunda, "Arctic summer sea ice could disappear as early as 2035," in *The National Geographic*, online, August 13, 2020, https://www.nationalgeographic.com/science/article/arctic-summer-sea-ice-could-be-

gone-by-2035 (Accessed: May 6, 2022).

9 "Pakistan, although only contributing 0.9% to global greenhouse gas (GHG) emissions, is one of the most vulnerable countries to the impacts of climate change. These impacts are primarily in the form of intense flooding, drastic change in rainfall patterns, melting Himalayan glaciers, increasing cases of vector-borne diseases such as dengue, and an overall increase in the frequency and intensity of climate-induced natural disasters. Climate Change imposes numerous challenges, and is becoming an existential threat globally. Pakistan's experience through Nature-based Solutions (NbS) in addressing the global challenges serves as a solution provider. Pakistan has surpassed mitigation contributions, and has taken climate change 'beyond Nationally Determined Contributions (NDCs), and took initiatives which contributed to reduction of 8.7% emissions between 2016-2018." Updated Nationally Determined Contributions, 2021 (Islamabad: Government of Pakistan, 2021), 12.

10 For details see Abinash Mohanty and Shreya Wadhawan, *Mapping India's Climate Vulnerability: A District Level Assessment* (New Delhi: Council on Energy, Environment and Water, 2021).

11 This problem has been recently been taken up at length in Roman Krznaric, *The Good Ancestor: A Radical Prescription for Long-Term Thinking* (New York: The Experiment, 2020).

Chapter I: Lessons for Our Final Century from Ibn Khaldun, Malthus, Mill, and Darwin

1 Ibn Khaldun, *The Muqaddimah* (An Introduction to History), trans.Franz Rosenthal, ed., N. J. Dawood (London: Routledge and Kegan Paul, 1978): 5.

2 According to the Environment Protection Agency (EPA), as of 2018, only 8.7% of plastics are recycled in the United States. https://www.epa.gov/facts-and-figures-about-materials-waste-and-recycling/plastics-material-specific-data (Accessed: May 6, 2022).

3 This projection has been accepted by the United Nations as of 2019. https://www.un.org/pga/73/2019/06/05/op-ed-we-must-save-our-world-from-drowning-in-plastic/ (Accessed: May 6, 2022).

4 This said, "Two-thirds of Americans are willing to pay more for everyday items made out of environmentally sustainable materials instead of single-use plastic, according to a survey from PBS NewsHour and Marist Poll." https://www.pbs.org/newshour/nation/most-americans-would-pay-more-to-avoid-using-plastic-poll-says (Accessed May 6, 2022). The problem is that the market is not willing to provide the alternatives as it knows that people will not sacrifice short-term convenience.

5 Paul Griffin, *The Carbon Majors Database: CDP Carbon Majors Report 2017*, (London: CDP, 2017), 6.

6 Tom Burgis, *Kleptopia: How Dirty Money Is Conquering the World* (Glasgow: William Collins, 2020).

7 Thomas Robert Malthus, "An Essay on the Principle of Population," History of Economic Thought Books, *McMaster University Archive for the History of Economic Thought*, no. malthus1798 (1798), http://socserv.mcmaster.ca/econ/ugcm/3ll3/malthus/popu.txt (Accessed: February 21, 2022).

8 Prior to the Covid-19 pandemic, the first two decades of the 21st century saw continued increase in average lifespan: "Globally, life expectancy has increased by more than 6 years between 2000 and 2019 – from 66.8 years in 2000 to 73.4 years in 2019. While healthy life expectancy (HALE) has also increased by 8% from 58.3 in 2000 to 63.7, in 2019, this was due to declining mortality rather than reduced years lived with disability." https://www.who.int/data/gho/data/themes/mortality-

and-global-health-estimates/ghe-life-expectancy-and-healthy-life-expectancy (Accessed: May 6, 2022). See, for instance, *Levels and Trends of Mortality since 1950: A Joint Study by the United Nations and World Health Organisation* (New York: United Nations, 1982) for the gains between 1950 and 1980.

[9] Jason Hickel, "Why Growth Can't be Green," *Jason Hickel*, Blog, last modified September 14, 2018, https://www.jasonhickel.org/blog/2018/9/14/why-growth-cant-be-green (Accessed February 21, 2022).

[10] D. Giurco, E. Dominish, N. Florin, T. Watari and B. McLellan, "Requirements for Minerals and Metals for 100% Renewable Scenarios," In Teske S. (eds) *Achieving the Paris Climate Agreement Goals* (Springer, Cham, 2019), https://doi.org/10.1007/978-3-030-05843-2_11 (Accessed February 21, 2022).

[11] "GDP per capita, PPP (current international \$)," *World Bank Group,* https://data.worldbank.org/indicator/NY.GDP.PCAP.PP.CD (Accessed: May 6, 2022).

[12] The average for OECD member states is about 45,000 dollars (per capita income). https://data.worldbank.org/indicator/NY.GDP.PCAP.PP.CD?locations=OE (Accessed: May 6, 2022).

[13] For a comprehensive analysis of this phenomenon and the fake change peddled by the very wealthy see Anand Giridharadas, *Winners Take All: The Elite Charade of Changing the World* (London: Penguin, 2019).

[14] John Stuart Mill, *The Principles of Political Economy: With some of their applications to Social Philosophy*, Vol. II (London: Parker, Son, and Bourn, West Strand, 1871).

[15] Ibid., 325.

[16] Charles Darwin and Leonard Kebler, *On the origin of species by means of natural selection, or, The preservation of favoured races in the struggle for life,* (London: J. Murray, 1859) https://www.loc.gov/item/06017473/ (Accessed: February 21, 2022).

[17] Charles Darwin, *The Descent of Man, and Selection in Relation to Sex* (New York: D. Appleton and Company, 1871).

[18] Ashley Hammer, "99 percent of the Earth's Species are Extinct – But That's not the Worst of It," *Discovery* August 1, 2019, https://www.discovery.com/nature/99-Percent-Of-The-Earths-Species-Are-Extinct (Accessed: May 6, 2022).

[19] Blaise Pascal, *Pascal's Pensées* (New York: E. P. Dutton & Co., Inc., 1958): 51.

Chapter II: Growing to Oblivion: The Crisis of Economic Thought and Our Final Century

[1] Riaz Muhammad Khan, *Environment Service Sector: Climate Perspective* (Islamabad: Civil Society Coalition for Climate Change), 1.

[2] Jared M. Diamond, *Collapse: How Societies Choose to Fail or Succeed*, (New York: Viking, 2005).

[3] Yuval Noah Harari, *Homo Deus*, (New York :Harper, 2017).

[4] Peter Turchin, *Ultrasociety: How 10,000 Years of War Made Humans the Greatest Cooperators on Earth* (Chaplin, CT: Beresta Books, 2016).

[5] Adam Smith, *An Inquiry into the Nature and Causes of the Wealth of Nations*, ed. Edwin A. Seligman (London: J. M. Dent, 1901).

[6] Karl Marx, 1818-1883, *The Communist Manifesto*, (London; Chicago, Ill.: Pluto Press, 1996).

[7] John M Keynes, *The Economic Consequences of the Peace*, (London: Macmillan & Co., Limited,

1919).

8 M. Friedman and P. N. Snowden, *Capitalism and Freedom* (Chicago: University of Chicago Press, 2002).

9 Reference the rise of China see Martin Jacques, *When China Rules the World: The End of the Western World and the Rise of a new Global Order* (London: Penguin, 2012).

10 For a deeply researched account on race relations in the United States see Elliot G. Jaspin, *Buried in the Bitter Waters: The Hidden History of Racial Cleansing in America* (New York: Perseus Book Company, 2007).

11 Cameron Cooper, "6 Economists who Predicted the global financial crisis," *In The Black,* July 7, 2015, https://intheblack.cpaaustralia.com.au/economy/6-economists-who-predicted-the-global-financial-crisis-and-why-we-should-listen-to-them-from-now-on (Accessed: May 6, 2022).

12 Yanis Varoufakis, *Adults in the room: My Battle with Europe's Deep Establishment*, (London : The Bodley Head, 2017).

13 Renee Choo, "How Close Are We to Climate Tipping Points?," *Columbia Climate School*, last modified November 11, 2021, https://news.climate.columbia.edu/2021/11/11/how-close-are-we-to-climate-tipping-points/ (Accessed: February 21, 2022).

14 "Act Now," *Extinction Rebellion*, https://extinctionrebellion.uk/act-now/ (Accessed: February 24, 2022).

15 Jason Hickel, "Why Growth Can't be Green," *Foreign Policy,* online, September 12, 2018, https://foreignpolicy.com/2018/09/12/why-growth-cant-be-green/ (Accessed: May 6, 2022).

16 *The Carbon Footprint of Global Trade: Tackling Emissions from International Freight Transport* (Paris: International Transport Forum, 2015), 3.

17 Ibid.

18 The day on which humanity's consumption of resources exceeds what the Earth can naturally replenish is now known as "Earth Overshoot Day". In 2021, that day arrived on 19 July. Since 2000, the the number of days after which we are mining the environment unsustainably has continued to grow. For more see https://www.overshootday.org/about-earth-overshoot-day/ (Accessed: May 6, 2022).

19 Amanda Macias, "America has spent $6.4 trillion on wars in the Middle East and Asia since 2001, a new study says," *CNBC,* last modified November 20, 2019, https://www.cnbc.com/2019/11/20/us-spent-6point4-trillion-on-middle-east-wars-since-2001-study.html (Accessed: February 24, 2022).

20 Kenneth Haapla, "US Government Funding of Climate Change," *Climate Dollars* https://www.climatedollars.org/full-study/us-govt-funding-of-climate-change/ (Accessed: May 6, 2022).

21 At present, we need 1.75 Earths to sustain our present level of consumption. If everyone were to live like an American, that shoots up to 5.1 Earths. https://www.overshootday.org/how-many-earths-or-countries-do-we-need/ (Accessed: May 6, 2022).

Chapter III: Solon and Croesus: Why Humans are Terrible at Making Wise Decisions

1 Niccolo Machiavelli, *The Discourses*, trans. Leslie J. Walker, ed., Bernard Crick (London: Penguin 2003), 94.

2 Tacitus, *The Histories,* trans. Kenneth Wellesley, ed. Rhiannon Ash (London: Penguin, 2009), 13.

3 Shang Yang, *The Book of Lord Shang*, trans. J. J. L. Duyvendak (Hertfordshire: Wordsworth, 1998),

200.

4 Herodotus, *Herodotus : the Histories*, (London, Eng.; New York: Penguin Books, 1996).

5 Abul-Fazl 'Allami, The *'Ain-i-Akbari*, (New Delhi: Atlantic Publishers and Distributors Pvt Ltd, 2021); Abū al-Faẓl ibn Mubārak, Henry Blochmann, H. S. Jarrett, and Jadunath Sarkar, *The A'in-i Akbari by Abu'l-Fazl 'Allami,* trans. H. Blochmann, (Calcutta: Asiatic Society of Bengal, 1927).

6 Peter Turchin, "Blame rich, overeducated elites as our society frays," *Bloomberg,* November 20, 2013, https://www.bloomberg.com/opinion/articles/2013-11-20/blame-rich-overeducated-elites-as-our-society-frays (Accessed: March 2, 2022).

7 Some 14 billion dollars were spent by candidates in the 2020 US election cycle. William C. R. Horncastle, "The 2020 election was the most expensive in history, but campaign spending does not always lead to success", *London School of Economics,* Phelan US Centre, November 27, 2020, https://blogs.lse.ac.uk/usappblog/2020/11/27/the-2020-election-was-the-most-expensive-in-history-but-campaign-spending-does-not-always-lead-to-success/ (Accessed: May 6, 2022).

8 In Pakistan, the phenomenon of "electables", i.e. candidates with dynastic political influence in a locality that can swing that constituency towards whever party they associate with, remains a powerful factor in government formation.

9 Eli Watkins, "Rubio stands by accepting NRA contributions: 'People buy into my agenda'," *CNN*, February 22, 2018, https://edition.cnn.com/2018/02/21/politics/rubio-nra-money-cameron-kasky/index.html (Accessed: March 4, 2022).

10 In the United States, for instance, "moderate" Democrats have delayed legislation intended to integrate climate change response into COVID19 recovery. Anthony Zurcher, "Joe Manchin and Kirsten Sinema Blocking Biden's Climate Agenda", *BBC online,* October 28, 2021, https://www.bbc.com/news/world-us-canada-59060739 (Accessed: May 6, 2022).

11 Louise Rhind-Tutt, "Yes, Prime Minister proves how little changes in British politics," *INews*, June 14, 2017, https://inews.co.uk/culture/television/yes-prime-minister-little-changes-in-british-politics-72493 (Accessed: March 4, 2022).

12 Coral Davenport and Eric Lipton, "Trump Picks Scott Pruitt, Climate Change Denialist, to Lead E.P.A.," *NYTimes*, December 7, 2016, https://www.nytimes.com/2016/12/07/us/politics/scott-pruitt-epa-trump.html (Accessed: March 4, 2022).

13 Alexis de Tocqueville, *The Old Regime and the Revolution* (Chicago: University of Chicago Press, 1998).

14 Michael Burleigh, *Sacred Causes: The Clash of Religion and Politics, from the Great War to the War on Terror* (New York: HarperCollins, 2007).

15 For a powerful corrective to this view see Mariana Mazzucato, *Mission Economy: A Moonshot Guide to Changing Capitalism* (London: AllenLane, 2021). Mazzucato explains how most of the critical innovations that define modern capitalism came from the government acting as a strategic investor, not from the creativity or competition of the free market and the entrepreneur. See also Piergiussepe Fortunato, "The Long Shadow of Market Fundamentalism", *Social Europe*, online, May 5, 2022, https://socialeurope.eu/the-long-shadow-of-market-fundamentalism (Accessed: May 6, 2022).

16 Jake Strumer and Yumi Asada, "Japan forced to confront resistance to immigration amid desperate labour shortage", *Australian Broadcasting Corporation*, online, December 20, 2018, https://www.abc.net.au/news/2018-12-20/japan-foreign-immigration-amid-desperate-labour-

shortage/10632288 (Accessed: May 6, 2022).

[17] Kartik Raj, "How Nativist Populism is going Mainstream in Europe", in *Human Rights Watch*, online, February 21, 2020. https://www.hrw.org/news/2020/02/21/how-nativist-populism-going-mainstream-europe (Accessed: May 6, 2022).

[18] Donella H Meadows, Dennis L. Meadows, Jørgen Randers, and William Behrens, *The Limits to growth; a report for the Club of Rome's project on the predicament of mankind* (New York: Universe Books, 1972).

[19] Noah Kirsch, "The 3 Richest Americans Hold More Wealth Than Bottom 50% Of The Country, Study Finds," *Forbes*, November 8, 2017. https://www.forbes.com/sites/noahkirsch/2017/11/09/the-3-richest-americans-hold-more-wealth-than-bottom-50-of-country-study-finds/?sh=3514bdda3cf8 (Accessed: March 4, 2022).

[20] "What is your Ecological Footprint?," *Global Footprint Network*, June 6, 2022, https://www.footprintcalculator.org/home/en.

[21] "Few concepts have implications as far reaching for economic policy as long-term growth. Growth– namely, the increase in an economy's potential to produce goods and services–is of central importance not only for improving living standards, but also for addressing inequality, debt sustainability, and the cost of climate change mitigation." *World Economic Outlook: Recovery during a Pandemic* (Washington D.C.: International Monetary Fund, Oct. 2021), 65.

[22] Kate Abnett, "Germany would have missed 2020 climate goal without COVID-19 emissions drop," *Reuters*, August 9, 2020. https://www.reuters.com/article/uk-climate-change-eu-germany-idUKKCN25F27F (Accessed: March 4, 2022).

[23] "A year ago, Open Lux uncovered the secrets of tax havens existing in Europe. Eight months later, the bombshell of the Pandora Papers made headlines around the world for blowing the lid on how the super-rich use tax havens to escape their tax bills. This week, a historic leak of Swiss banking records revealed how criminals, fraudsters and corrupt politicians used the secretive Swiss banking system to stash over $8 billion in assets. Yet, none of this made a dent in EU rules on tax havens. The updated list does not challenge the persistent weaknesses of the process which exempts EU tax havens, and leaves secrecy jurisdictions, like Switzerland and the US, and zero tax rate countries, like the Cayman Islands, off the hook. Meanwhile, poorer countries, like Tunisia and Vietnam, are at risk of being blacklisted for not complying with top-down designed standards. Greylisting the Bahamas, Bermuda and the British Virgin Islands means some real tax havens will be put under the magnifying glass. However, as long as the criteria are not reviewed, these countries can continue to operate as tax havens without any repercussions and can easily be completely delisted in the next review.

How many more tax scandals must happen before the EU commits to a real reform? The current process is full of holes, lacks credibility and fails to put an end to tax avoidance. It is time for the EU to automatically blacklist zero and low tax rate countries, and to hold EU countries up to the same level of scrutiny as non-EU countries. The EU should also not use the blacklist in the future to force poorer countries, like Nigeria and Kenya, to sign up to the unfair OECD tax deal," Chiara Putatoro, *Oxfam* ,Press Release, February 24, 2022, https://www.oxfam.org/en/press-releases/eu-countries-fall-short-their-promises-stop-tax-havens (Accessed: May 6, 2022).

[24] M. Ericsson, O. Löf and A. Löf, "Chinese control over African and global mining–past, present and future," *Miner Econ* 33 (2020): 153–181, https://doi.org/10.1007/s13563-020-00233-4 (Accessed:

March 4, 2022).

[25] Matthew Rochat, "China's Growing Dominance in Maritime Shipping," *The Diplomat*, December 18, 2021, https://thediplomat.com/2021/12/chinas-growing-dominance-in-maritime-shipping/ (Accessed: March 4, 2022).

[26] Junhua Zhang, "What's driving China's One Belt, One Road initiative?," *East Asia Forum*, September 2, 2016, https://www.eastasiaforum.org/2016/09/02/whats-driving-chinas-one-belt-one-road-initiative/ (Accessed: March 4, 2022).

[27] Christiane Grefe, "Interview with Dennis Meadows on "Limits to Growth"," *Volkswagen Foundation*, March 10, 2014, Youtube video, 23:21, https://youtu.be/uYNlhjOZ7DU?t=1401 (Accessed: March 4, 2022).

Chapter IV: The Pangloss Effect: Why Optimism is Lethal

[1] Abu'l-Fazl Allami, *The A'in- I Akbari*, trans. H. Blochmann, ed. D.C. Phillott (Lahore:Sang-e-Meel, 2004), 1146.

[2] Adam Zamoyski, *Moscow* 1812: *Napoleon's Fatal March* (New York: HarperCollins, 2004), 130-131.

[3] Voltaire, *Candide* (New York: Boni & Liveright, Inc, 1918).

[4] Giambattista Vico, *The New Science*, 3rd ed. trans. Thomas Goddard Bergin and Max Harold Fisch (Ithaca: Cornell UP, 1948).

[5] Francis Wheen, *How Mumbo Jumbo Conquered the World* (New York: Public Affairs, 2004).

[6] A broad cultural term for English becoming the global Internet lingua franca, used here to refer to Anglicised or globalized elites the world over who can talk to each other more easily than to their own countrymen.

[7] Laura Paddison, "How the Rich are Driving Climate Change," *BBC Online*, October 28, 2021, https://www.bbc.com/future/article/20211025-climate-how-to-make-the-rich-pay-for-their-carbon-emissions (Accessed: May 6, 2022).

[8] Nadège Mougel, "World War I casualties," *Reperes,* 2011, http://www.centre-robert-schuman.org/userfiles/files/REPERES%20%E2%80%93%20module%201-1-1%20-%20explanatory%20notes%20%E2%80%93%20World%20War%20I%20casualties%20%E2%80%93%20EN.pdf (Accessed: March 7, 2020).

[9] The Influenza Pandemic of 1919-1921 was a direct result of the First World War and claimed 50 million additional lives by American Center for Disease Control estimates. https://www.cdc.gov/flu/pandemic-resources/1918-commemoration/1918-pandemic-history.htm (Accessed: May 6, 2022).

[10] The Editors of Encyclopaedia Britannica, "Revolutions of 1830," *Encyclopedia Britannica*, July 20, 2021, https://www.britannica.com/event/Revolutions-of-1830 (Accessed: March 7, 2022).

[11] Office of the Historian, "American Isolationism in the 1930s," *US Department of State*, https://history.state.gov/milestones/1937-1945/american-isolationism (Accessed: March 7, 2022).

[12] "5 bloodiest wars in world history," *India Today*, April 17, 2015, https://www.indiatoday.in/education-today/gk-current-affairs/story/5-worst-wars-in-history-of-the-world-249029-2015-04-17 (Accessed: March 7, 2022).

[13] Shannon Hall, "Exxon Knew about Climate Change almost 40 Years ago," *The Scientific American*, online, October 26, 2015, https://www.scientificamerican.com/article/exxon-knew-about-climate-change-almost-40-years-ago/ (Accessed: May 6, 2022).

14 "The $1.90-a-day line is "obscenely low," and "earning $2 per day doesn't mean that you're somehow suddenly free of extreme poverty." A minimum of $7.40 per day, at least, is necessary for "basic nutrition and normal human life expectancy. Using the percentage of people in poverty is misleading, and we should instead focus on the absolute number of people in poverty, which according to Hickel's preferred $7.40-a-day line has *increased* since 1981." Jason Hickel, cited in Dylan Matthews, "Bill Gates Tweeted out a chart and sparked a huge debate about global poverty," *Vox*, February 12, 2019, https://www.vox.com/future-perfect/2019/2/12/18215534/bill-gates-global-poverty-chart (Accessed: May 6, 2022).

15 "6.7% Of World Has College Degree," *Huffington Post*, May 19, 2010, https://www.huffpost.com/entry/percent-of-world-with-col_n_581807 (Accessed: March 7, 2022).

16 Using constant 2017 USD, the global per capita income was about 11,000 in 2000. https://data.worldbank.org/indicator/NY.GNP.PCAP.PP.KD (Accessed: May 6, 2022).

17 "Pak-INDC," *UNFCCC*, November 4, 2016, https://www4.unfccc.int/sites/ndcstaging PublishedDocuments/Pakistan%20First/Pak-INDC.pdf; David Eckstein, Vera Künzel, Laura Schäfer and Maik Winges, *Global Climate Risk Index 2020*, (Bonn: GermanWatch, 2019): 9, https://www.germanwatch.org/sites/default/files/20-2-01e%20Global%20Climate%20Risk%20Index%20 2020_14.pdf (Accessed: March 7, 2022).

18 Muntazir Abbas, "India has 22 cars per 1,000 individuals: Amitabh Kant," *Auto: Economic Times,* December 12, 2018, https://auto.economictimes.indiatimes.com/news/passenger-vehicle/cars/india-has-22-cars-per-1000-individuals-amitabh-kant/67059021 (Accessed: March 7, 2022); David Banister, *Transport Planning: In the UK, USA and Europe* (London; New York: E & FN Spon, 1994), 193.

19 D. K. Panda, A. AghaKouchak, and S. K. Ambast, "Increasing heat waves and warm spells in India, observed from a multiaspect framework," *J. Geophys. Res. Atmos.*, no. 122 (2017): 3837–3858, doi:10.1002/2016JD026292 (Accessed March 7, 2022); Murali Krishnan, "Climate change: IPCC warns India of extreme heat waves, droughts," *DW*, August 10, 2018, https://www.dw.com/en/india-climate-change-ipcc/a-58822174 (Accessed March 7, 2022).

20 "What is net zero and why is it important?," *UN News*, December 02, 2020, https://news.un.org/en/story/2020/12/1078612 (Accessed: March 7, 2022).

21 Emily Gosden, "Eat seasonally and recycle more to cut emissions, says Shell," *The Times*, June 11, 2019, https://www.thetimes.co.uk/article/shell-asks-businesses-to-work-together-in-cutting-emissions-0pwkk2qnm (Accessed: March 7, 2022).

22 Tom Bawden, "Solar panel installations by homeowners and power companies plummet after subsidy cuts," *iNews*, November 04, 2020, https://inews.co.uk/news/environment/solar-panel-installations-homeowners-power-companies-plummet-749069 (Accessed: March 7, 2022).

23 Archana Rani,"Aker BP signs $1bn agreement with Maersk Drilling for two jack-up rigs," *Offshore Technology*, December 20, 2021, https://www.offshore-technology.com/news/aker-bp-maersk-drilling-rigs/ (Accessed: March 7, 2022).

24 Michelle R. McCrystall, Julienne Stroeve, Mark Serreze, Bruce C. Forbes and James A. Screen, "New climate models reveal faster and larger increases in Arctic precipitation than previously projected," *Nature Communications* 12, 6765 (2021): 3-10, https://doi.org/10.1038/s41467-021-27031-y (Accessed March 7, 2022).

25 Brian Resnick, "Melting permafrost in the Arctic is unlocking diseases and warping the landscape,"

Vox, November 15, 2019, https://www.vox.com/2017/9/6/16062174/permafrost-melting (Accessed: March 7, 2022).

[26] Justin Jin, "The workers searching for gas in the icy Russian Arctic – a photo essay," *The Guardian*, February 28, 2022, https://www.theguardian.com/artanddesign/2022/feb/28/wild-north-pioneers-on-energy-politics-coldest-battle-front-a-photo-essay-gazprom-arctic-siberia (Accessed: March 7, 2022).

[27] Ryan Burke, "Great-Power Competition in the "Snow of Far-Off Northern Lands": Why We Need a New Approach to Arctic Security," *Modern War Institute*, August 04, 2020, https://mwi.usma.edu/great-power-competition-snow-far-off-northern-lands-need-new-approach-arctic-security/ (Accessed: March 7, 2022).

[28] William Nordhaus, "Projections and Uncertainties about Climate Change in an Era of Minimal Climate Policies," *American Economic Journal: Economic Policy* 10, no. 3 (August 2008); Steve Keen, Nobel prize-winning economics of climate change is misleading and dangerous – here's why," T*he Conversation,* September 9, 2020, https://theconversation.com/nobel-prize-winning-economics-of-climate-change-is-misleading-and-dangerous-heres-why-145567 (Accessed: March 7, 2022).

[29] "Churchill and the Great Republic," *Library of Congress*, https://www.loc.gov/exhibits/churchill/wc-hour.html. (Accessed: March 7, 2022).

[30] Roy A. Austensen, "Metternich, Austria, and the German Question, 1848-1851," *The International History Review* 13, no. 1 (Feb., 1991): 21-37.

[31] Voltaire, An Essay on Universal History, the Manners, and Spirit of Nations: *From the Reign of Charlemaign to the Age of Lewis Xiv. - Primary Source Edition* (Sacramento: Creative Media Partners, LLC, 2014).

Chapter V: The Geopolitics of Climate Apocalypse

[1] Kautilya, *The Arthashastra,* trans., L. N. Rangarajan (New Delhi: Penguin Books, 1992), 559.

[2] Aytekin Demircioglu, "A Comparison of the Views of Ibn Khaldun and Montesquieu in Terms of the Effect of Climatic Conditions on Human Life," *The Anthropologist* 17: no. 3 (2014): 725-733, https://doi.org/10.1080/09720073.2014.11891486 (Accessed: March 9, 2022).

[3] James R. Hudson, "Braudel's Ecological Perspective," *Sociological Forum* 2, no. 1 (1987): 146-165, http://www.jstor.org/stable/684532 (Accessed: March 9, 2022).

[4] Jared Diamond, "Ecological Collapses of Past Civilizations,"*Proceedings of the American Philosophical Society* 38, no. 3 (363-370), https://www.jstor.org/stable/986741 (Accessed: March 9, 2022).

[5] Stephen W. Sawyer, "Time after Time: Narratives of the Longue Durée in the Anthropocene," *TransAtlantica*, no. 1 (2005), https://doi.org/10.4000/transatlantica.7344 (Accessed: March 9, 2022).

[6] James H. Lebovic, *Planning to Fail: The US Wars in Vietnam, Iraq, and Afghanistan*, (New York: Oxford University Press, 2019).

[7] Guillaume Simonet and Eric Duchemin, "The concept of adaptation : interdisciplinary scope and involvement in climate change," *Sapiens* 3, no. 1 (2010), https://journals.openedition.org/sapiens/997 (Accessed: March 9, 2022); T.F. Thornton, R.K. Puri, S. Bhagwat and Patricia Howard, "Human adaptation to biodiversity change: An adaptation process approach applied to a case study from southern India," *Ambio* 48, (2019): 1431–1446, https://doi.org/10.1007/s13280-019-01225-7

(Accessed: March 9, 2022).

[8] Natalie Novella, "How Humans Will End The World: A Cautionary History of Environmental and Civilizational Instability," *Inquiries Journal* 13, no. 09 (2021), http://www.inquiriesjournal.com/a?id=1905 (Accessed: March 9, 2022).

[9] Simon Dalby, *Anthropocene Geopolitics: Globalization, Security, Sustain.ability* (Ottawa: University of Ottawa Press, 2020).

[10] Krishan Kumar, "Colony and Empire, Colonialism and Imperialism: A Meaningful Distinction?," *Comparative Studies in Society and History* 63, no. 02 (2021): 280–309, https://doi.org/10.1017/S0010417521000050. See also Daniel Headrick, *Power over Peoples: Technology, Environments, and Western Imperialism, 1400* to Present (Princeton: Princeton University Press, 2010).

[11] Eugene Berger, George L. Israel, Charlotte Miller, Brian Parkinson, Andrew Reeves and Nadejda Williams, *World History: Cultures, States, and Societies to 1500* (Dahlonega: University of North Georgia Press, 2016).

[12] Kenneth Jupp, "European Feudalism from its Emergence through its Decline," *The American Journal of Economics and Sociology* 59, no. 05 (2000): 27-45.

[13] John Asafu-Adjaye, "Biodiversity Loss and Economic Growth: A Cross-Country Analysis," (paper presented at *Western Economic Association International,* Vancouver, B.C., 2000), 1-7.

[14] Stefano Guzzini (ed.), *The Return of Geopolitics in Europe? Social Mechanisms and Foreign Policy Identity Crises* (Cambridge: Cambridge University Press, 2012), 28.

[15] Shirley Cardenas, "How climate change could make some areas of Earth uninhabitable by 2500," *World Economic Forum*, October 21, 2021, https://www.weforum.org/agenda/2021/10/climate-change-could-make-some-areas-of-earth-uninhabitable-by-2500/ (Accessed: March 9, 2022).

[16] "Climate change likely led to fall of Indus Valley Civilisation, says Study," *The Hindu*, September 04, 2020, https://www.thehindu.com/sci-tech/energy-and-environment/climate-change-likely-led-to-fall-of-indus-valley-civilisation-says-study/article32521221.ece (Accessed: March 9, 2022).

[17] Carol Kerven, Sarah Robinson and Roy Behnke, "Pastoralism at Scale on the Kazakh Rangelands: From Clans to Workers to Ranchers," *Front. Sustain*. Food Syst. 4, no. 590401 (2021), https://doi.org/10.3389/fsufs.2020.590401 (Accessed: March 9, 2022).

[18] Brian Handwerk, "Little Ice Age Shrank Europeans, Sparked Wars," *National Geographic*, October 05, 2011, https://www.nationalgeographic.com/history/article/111003-science-climate-change-little-ice-age (Accessed: March 9, 2022).

[19] "The Black Death: The Plague, 1331-1770," *University of Iowa,* Accessed March 09, 2022, http://hosted.lib.uiowa.edu/histmed/plague/index.html (Accessed: March 9, 2022).

[20] Helle Abelvik-Lawson, "Cold weather and climate change explained," *Green Peace*, March 22, 2021, https://www.greenpeace.org.uk/news/cold-weather-and-climate-change-explained/ (Accessed: March 9, 2022); "Global warming makes heat waves hotter, longer, and more common," *National Academies*, August 23, 2021, https://www.nationalacademies.org/based-on-science/global-warming-makes-heat-waves-hotter-longer-and-more-common (Accessed: March 9, 2022).

[21] "Factsheet: Population trends in Asia and the Pacific," *UNSCAP*, November 2013, https://www.unescap.org/sites/default/files/SPPS-Factsheet-Population-Trends-v3.pdf (Accessed: March 9, 2022).

[22] In India, the top 1 per cent is presently assessed as owning nearly 60% of the country's wealth.

[23] Arguably, many communities are already in this condition.

24 Usman Kabir, "Heat waves in Pakistan, India could render urban areas unlivable: report," *Geo News,* January 17, 2020, https://www.geo.tv/latest/267822-heat-waves-in-pakistan-india-could-render-urban-areas-unlivable-contends-report (Accessed: March 9, 2022).

25 Already most population centres do not have a regular water supply.

26 The top consumer of water.

27 Guo Chushan, "Why human rights violations in Australia's offshore detention centers are appalling," *Global Times*, August 03, 2021, https://www.globaltimes.cn/page/202108/1230395.shtml (Accessed: March 9, 2022).

28 Shereen Marisol Meraji and Adrian Florido, Interview with Karen Ishizuka, *Code Switch Podcast*, NPR, July 03. 2019, https://www.npr.org/transcripts/738247414 (Accessed: March 9, 2022).

29 Marta Welander, "The Politics of Exhaustion and the Externalization of British Border Control. An Articulation of a Strategy Designed to Deter, Control and Exclude," *International Migration* 59, no. 03 (2021): 29-46, https://doi.org/10.1111/imig.12778 (Accessed: March 9, 2022).

30 Tim Hornyak, "Climate Change could make Siberia an attractive place to Live," *Eos*, online, July 12, 2017, https://eos.org/articles/climate-change-could-make-siberia-an-attractive-place-to-live (Accessed: May 6, 2022).

31 Jason Hickel, Dylan Sullivan and Huzaifa Zoomkawala, "Rich countries drained $152tn from the Global South since 1960," *Al Jazeera*, May 06, 2021, https://www.aljazeera.com/opinions/2021/5/6/rich-countries-drained-152tn-from-the-global-south-since-1960 (Accessed: March 9, 2022).

32 Emily Prey, "The United States Must Reckon With Its Own Genocides," *Foreign Policy*, October 11, 2021, https://foreignpolicy.com/2021/10/11/us-genocide-china-indigenous-peoples-day-columbus/(Accessed: March 9, 2022); Karen E. Smith, *Genocide and the Europeans*, (Cambridge: Cambridge University Press, 2010); R.J. Rummel, *Lethal Politics: Soviet Genocide and Mass Murder Since 1917,* (New Brunswick, N.J.: Transaction Publications, 1992).

33 Jilin Xu, "Social Darwinism in modern China," *Journal of Modern Chinese History* 6, no. 02 (2002): 182-197, https://doi.org/10.1080/17535654.2012.718605 (Accessed: March 9, 2022).

34 David o. Shullman, "Protect the Party: China's growing influence in the developing world," *Brookings*, January 22, 2019, https://www.brookings.edu/articles/protect-the-party-chinas-growing-influence-in-the-developing-world/ (Accessed: March 9, 2022); Tom Phillips, "World's biggest building project aims to make China great again," *The Guardian*, May 12, 2017, https://www.theguardian.com/world/2017/may/12/chinese-president-belt-and-road-initiative (Accessed: March 9, 2022).

35 Don Hinrichsen, "The Coastal Population Explosion," in *Trends and Future Challenges for U.S. National Ocean and Coastal Policy: August 1999*, edited by Biliana Cicin-Sain, Robert W. Knecht, and Nancy Foster (Delaware: Center for the Study of Marine Policy, 1999), 27-29.

36 Kenneth Waltz, "The Spread of Nuclear Weapons: More May Better," *Adelphi Papers*, no. 171 (London: International Institute for Strategic Studies, 1981)

Chapter VI: The Transience of High-Level Equilibrium and the Inevitability of Downfall

1 Edward Gibbon, *The Decline and Fall of the Roman Empire*, abridged, Frank C. Bourne (New York: Dell Publishing, 1963), 27.

2 "Herodotus Part 1 (Selection from Scroll 1)," trans. Lynn Sawlivich, Gregory Nagy, Claudia Filos,

Sarah Scott, and Keith Stone, *The Center for Hellenic Studies*, November 03, 2020, https://chs. harvard.edu/primary-source/herodotus-selections-part-i/ (Accessed: March 11, 2022).

[3] Paul Kennedy, *The Rise and Fall of Great Powers* (New York: Random House, 1987).

[4] Douglas Lemke, "The Continuation of History: Power Transition Theory and the End of the Cold War," *Journal of Peace Research* 34, no. 1 (Feb., 1997): 23-36, https://www.jstor.org/stable/424828 (Accessed: March 11, 2022).

[5] Hal Brands and Jake Sullivan, "China has two paths to global domination," *Foreign Affairs*, May 22, 2020, https://foreignpolicy.com/2020/05/22/china-superpower-two-paths-global-domination-cold-war/ (Accessed: March 11, 2022).

[6] Laying the foundation of the Pax Romana that followed his nephew's victory in the civil wars that erupted after his assassination.

[7] See, for instance, Amira K. Bennison, *The Great Caliphs: The Golden Age of the 'Abbasid Empire* (London: I.B. Tauris, 2011).

[8] See Philip Ball, *The Water Kingdom: A Secret History of China* (London: The Bodley Head, 2016).

[9] Barry L. Isaac, "Aztec Warfare: Goals and Battlefield Comportment," *Ethnology* 22, no. 2 (Apr., 1983): 121-131, https://doi.org/10.2307/3773575 (Accessed: March 11, 2022).

[10] Ira M. Lapidus, "The Evolution of Muslim Urban Society," *Comparative Studies in Society and History* 15, no. 1 (Jan., 1973): 21-50, https://www.jstor.org/stable/178186 (Accessed: March 11, 2022).

[11] Robin Blackburn, "The Old World Background to European Colonial Slavery," *The William and Mary Quarterly* 54, no. 1 (Jan., 1997): 65-102, https://doi.org/10.2307/2953313 (Accessed: March 11, 2022).

[12] "UTES - Energy and Economic Development: Understanding the Role of Hierarchy - Blair Fix," *Energy Institute, University of Texas at Austin,* 28 April, 2021, Youtube video, 59:11, https://www. youtube.com/watch?v=4YMnlypUiDY (Accessed: March 11, 2022).

[13] "Pyramids of Giza are central to Egypt's tourism recovery," *Travel Guard*, July 01, 2014, https:// www.travelguard.com/travel-news/pyramids-of-giza-are-central-to-egypts-tourism-recovery (Accessed: March 11, 2022).

[14] Alan B. Lloyd, "Herodotus' Account of Pharaonic History," *Historia: Journal of Ancient History 37*, no. 01 (1988): 22-53, https://www.jstor.org/stable/4436037 (Accessed: March 11, 2022).

[15] Actually a series of walls begun by the Qin dynasty.

[16] Fernão Mendes Pinto, *The Travels of Mendes Pinto,* (Chicago: University of Chicago Press, 1989), 221-222.

[17] "Past present: Decadence of the Mughal nobility," *DAWN*, October 18, 2009, https://www.dawn. com/news/883698/past-present-decadence-of-the-mughal-nobility (Accessed: March 11, 2022).

[18] John Madden, "Slavery in the Roman Empire Numbers and Origins," *Classics Ireland* 3 (1996): 109-128, https://doi.org/10.2307/25528294 (Accessed: March 11, 2022).

[19] "Britain and the Caribbean." *BBC*, https://www.bbc.co.uk/bitesize/guides/zjyqtfr/revision/6 (Accessed: March 11, 2022).

[20] J. R. Ward, "The Industrial Revolution and British Imperialism, 1750-1850," *The Economic History Review: New Series* 47, no. 1 (Feb., 1994): 44-65, https://doi.org/10.2307/2598220 (Accessed: March 11, 2022).

[21] Annie Jacobsen, *Operation Paperclip: The Secret Intelligence Program to Bring Nazi Scientists to*

America (New York: Little, Brown and Company, 2014).

[22] Stephen Dando-Collins, "Legions of Rome: Where It All Began," *The History Reader*, September 30, 2012, https://www.thehistoryreader.com/military-history/legions-rome-began/ (Accessed: March 11, 2022).

[23] Evan Andrews, "8 Ways Roads Helped Rome Rule the Ancient World," *History*, Updated April 15, 2021, https://www.history.com/.amp/news/8-ways-roads-helped-rome-rule-the-ancient-world (Accessed: March 11, 2022).

[24] For detailed examination of South Asian political economy see Taypan Raychaudhary and Irfan Habib, eds., *The Camrbidge Economic History of History, Vol. 1, c. 1200 to 1750* (Cambridge: Cambridge University Press, 1982).

[25] "Perhaps 10 percent of 75 million people living in the Roman Empire never recovered. 'Like some beast,' a contemporary wrote, the sickness 'destroyed not just a few people but rampaged across whole cities and destroyed them.'" Edward Watts, "What Rome Learnt from the Deadly Antonine Plague," *Smithsonian Magazine,* online, April 28, 2020, https://www.smithsonianmag.com/history/what-rome-learned-deadly-antonine-plague-165-d-180974758/ (Accessed: May 7, 2022).

[26] They would never be the same again after the trauma they endured between 1200-1400.

[27] P. Jackson, "The Mongols and the Delhi Sultanate in the Reign of Muḥammad Tughluq (1325–1351)," *Central Asiatic Journal* 19, no. 1/2 (1975): 118-157, https://www.jstor.org/stable/41927097 (Accessed: March 11, 2022).

[28] Jean Johnson, "The Mongol Dynasty: When Kublai Khan Ruled China," *Asian Society*, Accessed March 11, 2022, https://asiasociety.org/education/mongol-dynasty (Accessed: March 11, 2022).

[29] Ian Morris, *Why the West Rules – For Now: The Patterns of History and What they Reveal About the Future* (Profile Books: London, 2010).

[30] Robert L. Bloom, Basil L. Crapster and Harold A. Dunkelberger, "1. The Heirs of the Roman Empire: Byzantium, Islam, and Medieval Europe. Pt. II: Medieval, Political, and Economic Development: Feudalism and Manorialism, " In *Ideas and Institutions of Western Man* (Gettysburg: Gettysburg College, 1958), 1-6.

[31] See, for instance, A. C. Grayling, *The Age of Genius: The Seventeenth Century and the Birth of the Modern Mind* (London: Bloomsbury, 2016), which examines the eventual, though not inevitable, triumph of the humanist legacy.

[32] For a classic history of the Spanish overseas empire see C. H. Haring, *The Spanish Empire in America* (New York: Harbinger Books, 1963).

[33] S. O. Becker, S. Pfaff and J. Rubin, "Causes and consequences of the Protestant Reformation," *ESI* Working Paper 16-13 (2016): 1-44, http://digitalcommons.chapman.edu/esi_working_papers/178 (Accessed: March 11, 2022).

[34] David Wootton, The Invention of Science: *A New History of the Scientific Revolution* (New York: Harper Collins, 2015).

[35] For a now classic but still relevant analysis of the economic basis for slavery in the Atlantic world and its inextricable relationship with the rise of modern capitalism see Eric Williams, *Capitalism & Slavery* (Chapel Hill: University of North Carolina Press, 1945): esp., 3-29,

[36] John Breuilly, (ed.) *The Oxford Handbook of the History of Nationalism* (Oxford: Oxford University Press, 2013), 832.

[37] Amina Khan, "How much Arctic sea ice are you melting? Scientists have an answer," *Los Angeles*

Times, November 03, 2016, https://www.latimes.com/science/sciencenow/la-sci-sn-co2-sea-ice-20161103-story.html (Accessed: March 11, 2022).

[38] Lizzy Gurdus, "Boeing CEO: Over 80% of the world has never taken a flight. We're leveraging that for growth," *CNBC*, December 07, 2017, https://www.cnbc.com/2017/12/07/boeing-ceo-80-percent-of-people-never-flown-for-us-that-means-growth.html (Accessed: March 11, 2022).

[39] "Facts & Figures," *ATAG*, https://www.atag.org/facts-figures.html (Accessed: March 11, 2022).

[40] "Global wealth inequalities are even more pronounced than income inequalities. The poorest half of the global population barely owns any wealth at all, possessing just 2% of the total. In contrast, the richest 10% of the global population own 76% of all wealth. On average, the poorest half of the population owns PPP €2,900 per adult, i.e. USD4,100 and the top 10% own €550,900 (or USD771,300) on average," *World Inequality Report* (2022), online, https://wir2022.wid.world/executive-summary/ (Accessed: May 7, 2022).

[41] "During this same 20-year period of increased reporting and sustainable investing, carbon emissions have continued to rise, and environmental damage has accelerated. Social inequity, too, is increasing. For example, in the United States the gap between median CEO compensation and median worker pay has widened, even though public companies are now required to disclose that ratio." Kenneth P. Pucker, "Overselling Sustainability Reporting," *Harvard Business Review*, online, May/June 2021, https://hbr.org/2021/05/overselling-sustainability-reporting (Accessed: May 7, 2022).

Chapter VII: Orders of Darkness: Government and Post-Government Amidst the Ruins

[1] Quoted by Michael Axworthy in *Empire of the Mind: A History of Iran* (London: Hurst & Company, 2007).

[2] Omar Khayyam, *The Rubaiyat*, trans. Edward Fitzgerald (London: Collins, 1947), 104.

[3] John Rapley, "The New Middle Ages: Gangsters' Paradise," *Foreign Affairs*, May/June 2006, https://www.foreignaffairs.com/articles/2006-05-01/new-middle-ages (Accessed: March 14, 2022); Kristin Baird Rattini, "Who was Constantine?," *National Geography*, February 25, 2019, https://www.nationalgeographic.com/culture/article/constantine (Accessed: March 14, 2022).

[4] Collin Rickets, "The Growth of Christianity in the Roman Empire," *History Hit*, August 9, 2018, https://www.historyhit.com/the-growth-of-christianity-in-the-roman-empire/ (Accessed: March 14, 2022).

[5] Saint Augustine, *City of God*, edited by G. R. Evans, trans. Henry Bettenson (London: Penguin Books, 2003).

[6] Sean McGlynn, *Kill Them All: Cathars and Carnage in the Albigensian Crusade* (Stroud: The History Press, 2015).

[7] John Van Engen, "The Future of Medieval Church History," *Church History* 71, no. 3 (Sep., 2002): 492-522, https://www.jstor.org/stable/4146417 (Accessed: March 14, 2022).

[8] Gemma Betros, "The French Revolution and the Catholic Church," *History Review*, no. 68 (December 2010) https://www.historytoday.com/archive/french-revolution-and-catholic-church (Accessed: March 14, 2022); Alexa Weight, "God and Revolution: Religion and Power from Pre-Revolutionary France to the Napoleonic Empire" *Student Theses, Papers and Projects (History)* 64 (2017): 1-51, https://digitalcommons.wou.edu/his/64 (Accessed: March 14, 2022).

[9] See, for instance, John Gray, *Black Mass: Apocalyptic Religion and the Death of Religion* (New York: Farrar, Straus and Giroux, 2008).

[10] For a classic work on how this process works see Wilhelm Reich, *The Mass Psychology of Fascism* (Lahore: Gautam 1995; FP New York: Orgone Institute Press, 1946).

[11] Such as Google, Apple, Amazon, Facebook, Twitter, etc.

[12] "Fitness app Strava lights up staff at military bases," *BBC*, January 29, 2008, https://www.bbc.com/news/technology-42853072 (Accessed: March 14, 2022).

[13] Giovanni Luca Ciampaglia and Filippo Menczer, "Biases Make People Vulnerable to Misinformation Spread by Social Media," *Scientific American,* June 21, 2018, https://www.scientificamerican.com/article/biases-make-people-vulnerable-to-misinformation-spread-by-social-media/ (Accessed: March 15, 2022).

[14] See, for instance, Gary Machado Alexandre Alaphillippe, Roman Adamczyk, and Antoine Grégorie, *Indian Chronicles: Deep Dive into a 15-Year Operation Targeting the EU and UN to Serve Indian Interests* (EU Disinfor Lab, 2020).

[15] Meg Jing Zeng, "China's Social Credit System puts its people under pressure to be model citizens," *The Conversation*, January 23, 2018, https://theconversation.com/chinas-social-credit-system-puts-its-people-under-pressure-to-be-model-citizens-89963 (Accessed: March 15, 2022).

[16] Christopher Soelistyo, "Artificial Intelligence: The Technology of Social Control?," *Science Innovation Union,* January 6, 2021, http://science-union.org/articlelist/2021/1/6/artificial-intelligence-the-technology-of-social-control (Accessed: March 15, 2022).

[17] Jen Clark, "What is the Internet of Things (IoT)?," *IBM*, November 17, 2016, https://www.ibm.com/blogs/internet-of-things/what-is-the-iot/ (Accessed: March 15, 2022).

[18] Shoshana Zuboff, *The Age of Surveillance Capitalism: The Fight for a Human Future at the New Frontier of Power* (New York: Public Affairs, 2019).

[19] Aldous Huxley, *Brave New World* (New York: Harper Brothers, 1932); Suzanne Collins, *The Hunger Games* (New York: Scholastic, 2008).

[20] James Q. Whitman, "Of Corporatism, Fascism, and the First New Deal," *The American Journal of Comparative Law 39*, no. 4 (Autumn, 1991): 747-778, https://doi.org/10.2307/840740 (Accessed: March 15, 2022).

Conclusion

[1] Han Suyin, *Eldest Son: Zhou Enlai and the Making of Modern China,* 1878-1976 (London: Random House, 1994), 90.

SELECT BIBLIOGRAPHY

Arberry, A. J. ed. *The Legacy of Persia.* London: Oxford University Press, 1968.

Asprey, Robert. *The Rise and Fall of Napoleon Bonaparte* Vol. II, The Fall. London: Abacus, 2002.

Axworthy, Michael. *Empire of the Mind: A History of Iran.* London: Hurst & Company, 2007.

________. *The Sword of Persia: Nader Shah, from Tribal Warrior to Conquering Tyrant.* London: I. B. Tauris, 2009.

Ball, Philip. *The Water Kingdom: A Secret History of China.* London: The Bodley Head, 2016.

Bayly, C. A. *The Birth of the Modern World: 1780-1914.* Oxford: Blackwell Publishing, 2004.

Becher, Matthias. *Charlemagne.* London: Yale University Press, 2003.

Birnbaum, Pierre. *The Idea of France.* Trans. M. B. DeBevoise. New York: Hill and Wang, 2001.

Blanning, T. C. W. *The Culture of Power and the Power of Culture: Old Regime Europe 1660-1789.* Oxford: Oxford University Press, 2002.

Braudel, Ferdinand. *A History of Civilizations.* Trans. Richard Mayne. New York: Penguin Group, 1995.

________. *Civilization and Capitalism 15th-18th Century.* Trans. Sian Reynolds. Vol I.

________. *The Structures of Everyday Life.* London: Phoenix Press, 2002.

________. Vol. II. *The Wheels of Commerce.* London: Phoenix Press, 2002.

________. Vol. III. *The Perspective of the World.* London: Phoenix Press, 2002.

Burke, Edmund. *Reflections on the Revolutions in France,* ed. J. C. D. Clark. Stanford: Stanford University Press, 2001.

Burleigh, Michael. *Earthly Powers: Religion and Politics in Europe from the Enlightenment to the Great War.* London: HarperCollins Publishers, 2005.

________. *The Third Reich: A New History.* London: Macmillan, 2000.

Buruma, Ian. *Voltaire's Coconuts or Anglomania in Europe.* London, Phoenix, 2000.

Carr, Matthew. *Blood and Faith: The Purging of Muslim Spain.* London: Hurst & Company, 2017.

Cicero. *The Republic and The Laws.* Trans. Niall Rudd. Oxford: Oxford University Press, 2008.

Clements, Jonathan. *The First Emperor of China.* Gloucestershire: Sutton

Publishing, 2004.

Clausewitz, Carl von. *On War.* Trans., Michael Howard and Peter Paret. Princeton: Princeton University Press, 1989.

Darwin, Charles. *On the Origins of Species.* London: GlobalGrey, 2019.

Darwin, John. *After Tamerlane: The Global History of Empire since 1405.* London: Penguin Books, 2007.

Davidson, Ian. Voltaire in Exile: The Last Years, 1753 – 78. London: Atlantic Books, 2004.

Diamond, Jared. *Collapse: How Societies Choose to Fail or Succeed.* New York: Viking, 2005.

Dower, John. *Embracing Defeat: Japan in the Wake of World War II.* New York: W. W. Norton & Company, The New Press, 1999.

Ferguson, Niall. Empire: How Britain Made the Modern World. London: The Penguin Press, 2003.

________. *Civilization: The West and the Rest.* London: Allen Lane, the Penguin Press, 2011.

Feuchtwanger, Edgar. *Bismarck.* New York: Routledge, 2003.

Fischel, Walter J. *Ibn Khaldun in Egypt: His Public Functions and his Historical Research, A Study in Islamic Historiography.* Berkeley: University of California Press, 1967.

Fukuyama, Francis. *The Origins of Political Order: From Prehuman Times to the French Revolution.* London: ProPile Books, 2012.

________. *Trust: The Social Virtues and the Creation of Prosperity.* New York: The Free Press, 1995.

Giridharadas, Anand. *Winners Take All: The Elite Charade of Changing the World.* London: Penguin, 2019

Gibbon, Edward. *The Decline and Fall of the Roman Empire.* Abridged and with an Introduction by Frank C. Bourne. New York: Dell Publishing Co., 1963.

Goff, Jacques Le. *Medieval Civilization: 400–1500,* trans. Julia Barrow. Oxford: Basil Blackwell, 1984.

Goody, Jack. *The Eurasian Miracle.* Cambridge: Polity Press, 2010.

Grant, Michael. T*he Fall of the Roman Empire.* London: Phoenix, 2005.

Gray, John. Black Mass: *Apocalyptic Religion and the Death of Utopia.* New York: Farrar, Straus and Giroux, 2007.

Grayling, A. C. *The Age of Genius: The Seventeenth Century and the Birth of the Modern Mind (*London: Bloomsbury, 2016.

Haring, C. H. *The Spanish Empire in America.* New York: Harbinger Books, 1963.

Headrick, Daniel R. *Power over Peoples: Technology, Environments, and Western Imperialism, 1400 to Present.* Princeton: Princeton University Press, 2010.

Herodotus. *Histories.* Trans. George Rawlinson. Hertfordshire: Wordsworth Editions, 1996.

Hill, Charles. *Grand Strategies: Literature, Statecraft and World Order.* New Haven: Yale University Press, 2010.

Hitchcock, Montgomery, F. R. St. *Augustine's Treatise on the City of God.* New York: The MacMillan Company, 1922.

Ibn Khaldun. *The Muqaddimah (An Introduction to History).* Trans. Franz Rosenthal. Ed., N. J. Dawood. London: Routledge and Kegan Paul, 1978.

Judt, Tony. Postwar: *A History of Europe since 1945.* London: William Heineman, 2005.

Kaplan, Robert D. T*he Revenge of Geography: What the Map tells us about Coming Conflicts and the Battle against Fate.* New York: Random House, 2012.

Katouzian, Homa. *The Political Economy of Modern Iran: Despotism and PseudoModernism, 1926-1979.* London: MacMillan, 1981.

__________. *State and Society in Iran: The Eclipse of the Qajars and the Emergence of the Pahlavis.* London: I. B. Tauris Publishers, 2000.

Kautilya. *The Arthashastra*, trans, L. N. Rangarajan. New Delhi: Penguin Books, 1992.

__________. *The Arthashastra*, trans, R. Shamasastry. Bangalore: Government Press, 1915.

Kennedy, Hugh. *The Court of the Caliphs: When Baghdad Ruled the Muslim World.* London: Phoenix, 2005.

Kennedy, Paul. *The Rise and Fall of the Great Powers: Economic Change and Military Conflict 1500-2000.* London: Fontana Press, 1989.

Kemp, Barry J. *Ancient Egypt: Anatomy of a Civilization.* London: Routledge, 2002.

Kissinger, Henry. *Diplomacy.* New York: Simon & Schuster, 1994.

__________. *On China.* Penguin: London, 2012.

Krznaric, Roman. *The Good Ancestor: A Radical Prescription for Long-Term Thinking.* New York: The Experiment, 2020.

Machiavelli, Niccolo. *The Discourses.* Trans. Leslie J. Walker. Ed. Bernard Crick. Rev. Brian Richardson. London: Penguin Books, 2003.

MacMullen, Ramsay *Corruption and the Decline of Rome.* New Haven: Yale

University Press, 1988.

Malthus, Thomas. *An Essay on the Principle of Population*. London: J. Johnson, 1798.

Marx. Karl. Capital: *A New Abridgement*. Ed. David McLellan. London: Oxford University Press, 2008.

Massie, Robert K. *Peter the Great: His Life and World*. London: Cardinal, 1989.

Mastutani Akihiko. *Shrinking Population Economics: Lessons from Japan*. Trans. Brian Miller. Tokyo: International House of Japan, 2006.

Meadows, Donella, Dennis Meadows, Jørgen Randers, and William W. Behrens III. *The Limits to Growth: A Report for the Club of Rome's Project on the Predicament of Mankind*. New York: Universe Books, 1972.

Friedman, Milton. *Capitalism and Freedom*. Chicago: University of Chicago Press, 1962.

Niaz, Ilhan. *Old World Empires: Cultures of Power and Governance in Eurasia*. New York: Routledge, 2014.

Moore, Barrington Jr. *Social Origins of Dictatorship and Democracy: Lord and Peasant in the Making of the Modern World*. Boston: Beacon Press, 1967.

Morris, Ian. *Why the West Rules—for Now: The Patterns of History and What they Reveal about the Future*. London: ProFile Books, 2010.

Perdue, Leo G. *The Sword and the Stylus: An Introduction to Wisdom in the Age of Empires*. Grand Rapids: Wm. B. Eerdmans Publishing Co., 2008.

Pipes, Richard. *Property and Freedom*. New York: Alfred A. Knopf, 1999.

Plato. *Dialogues of Plato*. Trans. Benjamin Jowett. Ed. Cynthia Brantley Johnson. New York: Simon & Schuster, 2010.

Plutarch. *The Rise and Fall of Athens: Nine Greek Lives*. Trans. Ian Scott-Kilvert. London: Penguin Books, 1965.

Possehl, Gregory ed. *Harappan Civilization: A Contemporary Perspective*. New Delhi: Oxford and IBH Publishing Co., 1982.

Raychaudhary, Taypan and Irfan Habib, eds. *The Cambridge Economic History of History, Vol. 1, c. 1200 to 1750*. Cambridge: Cambridge University Press, 1982.

Redman, Ben Ray, ed. *The Portable Voltaire*. New York: Viking Penguin Inc., 1977.

Reich, Wilhelm. T*he Mass Psychology of Fascism*. Lahore: Gautam 1995.

Roberts, Andrew. *Hitler and Churchill: Secrets of Leadership*. London: Phoenix, 2003.

Roberts, J. M. *History of the World*. New York: Oxford University Press, 1993.

Russel, Bertrand. *Power: A New Social Analysis.* London: Unwin Books, 1960.

Sale, Kirkpatrick. *The Conquest of Paradise: Christopher Columbus and the Columbian Legacy.* New York: Alfred A. Knopf, 1991.

Secondat, Charles de. *The Spirit of Laws.* New York: Prometheus Books, 2002.

Sen, Amartya. *Identity and Violence: The Illusion of Destiny.* New York: W. W. Norton and Company, 2006.

Shang Yang. *The Book of Lord Shang.* Trans. J. J. L. Duyvendak. Intro. Robert Wilkinson. Hertfordshire: Wordsworth Editions Limited, 1998.

Siedentop, Larry. *Democracy in Europe.* London: Allen Lane Penguin Press, 2000.

Skinner, Quentin. *Visions of Politics.* Vol. I, Regarding Method. Cambridge: Cambridge University Press, 2002.

________. Visions of Politics. Vol. II, *Renaissance Virtues.* Cambridge: Cambridge University Press, 2002.

________. Visions of Politics. Vol. III, *Hobbes and Civil Science.* Cambridge: Cambridge University Press, 2002.

Smith, Adam. *An Inquiry into the Nature and Causes of the Wealth of Nations.* Philadelphia: Pennsylvania State University Electronics Classics Series Publication, 2005.

Spellman, W. M. *Monarchies: 1000-2000.* London: Reaktion Books, 2001.

Standage, Tom. *An Edible History of Humanity.* New York: Walbert Company, 2009.

Tacitus. *The Annals: The Reigns of Tiberius, Claudius, and Nero*, trans. J. C. Yardley. Oxford: Oxford University Press, 2008.

Tocqueville, Alexis de. *Democracy in America.* Trans. George Lawrence. Ed., J. P. Mayer. New York: HarperCollins, 2000.

________. *The Old Regime and the Revolution.* Trans. Alan S. Kahan. Edited and with an Introduction by François Furet and Françoise Mélonio. Chicago: University of Chicago Press, 1998.

Toynbee, Arnold J. *A Study of History.* Abridged in two volumes by D. C. Somervell New York: Dell Publishing Co., 1978.

Tusi, Nizam-ul-Mulk. *The Book of Government or Rules for Kings: The Siyasatnama or Siyar al-Muluk of Nizam al-Mulk.* Trans. Hubert Drake. London: Routledge and Kegan Paul, 1960.

Vico, Giambattista. *The New Science.* Trans. Thomas Goddard Bergin and Max Harold Fisch. Ithaca: Cornell University Press, 1948.

Volkogonov, Dmitri. *The Rise and Fall of the Soviet Empire: Political Leaders from Lenin to Gorbachev.* Trans. Harold Shukman. London: HarperCollins, 1999.

Weber, Max. *The Protestant Ethic and the Spirit of Capitalism.* Trans. Talcott Parsons. New York: Charles Scribner's Sons, 1950.

Wheen, Francis. *How Mumbo-Jumbo Conquered the World: A Short History of Modern Delusions.* London: The Fourth Estate, 2004.

Williams, Eric. *Capitalism & Slavery.* Chapel Hill: University of North Carolina Press, 1945.

Wittfogel, Karl A. *Oriental Despotism: A Comparative Study of Total Power.* New Haven: Carl Purington Rollins Printing Office of the Yale University Press, 1963.

Zimbardo, Philip. *The Lucifer Effect: How Good People Turn Evil.* London: Rider, 2007.

About the Author

Ilhan Niaz is the author of *The State During the British Raj: Imperial Governance in South Asia, 1700-1947* (OUP, 2019), *Old World Empires: Cultures of Power and Governance in Eurasia* (Routledge/OUP, 2014), *The Culture of Power and Governance of Pakistan, 1947-2008* (OUP 2010), and *An Inquiry into the Culture of Power of the Subcontinent* (Alhamra, 2006). He has been published in leading international academic journals, including *The Round Table, The Journal of the Royal Asiatic Society, Asian Affairs* (The Journal of the Royal Society for Asian Affairs), *Asian Profile, The New Zealand Journal of Asian Studies, South Asia: Journal of South Asian Studies*, and *The Journal of South Asian and Middle Eastern Studies*. He also occasionally contributes articles and reviews to leading national news publications. *The Culture of Power and Governance of Pakistan* was awarded the best non-fiction book of 2010 at the 2011 Karachi Literature Festival and has also received the Higher Education Commission of Pakistan award for best book in social sciences, arts and humanities for 2010. *Old World Empires: Cultures of Power and Governance in Eurasia* received the HEC award for best book in social sciences for 2013/14. *The State During the British Raj* received the 2021 HEC award for Best Book publication. He is also the recipient of the Kodikara Award for 2013 (RCSS, Colombo) and has, in connection with that award, authored a monograph on *Understanding and Addressing the Administrative Aspect of the Civil-Military Imbalance* in Pakistan. He is presently Professor of History at the Quaid-i-Azam University, Islamabad.

Centre for Strategic and Contemporary Research presents fresh and original takes in digital and print formats on matters of concern for a diverse set of public and civil society stakeholders.

We explore avenues of research, consultancy, and advocacy. The team at the Centre helps targeted segments understand the policy choices facing Pakistan and the rest of the world.

The Centre continues to play an active part in ushering a positive perceptual shift within our audience.